EDUCATION OF AN AMBASSADOR

EDUCATION OF AN AMBASSADOR

Reflections on Higher Education Reform in Kerala

TP Sreenivasan

KONARK PUBLISHERS PVT LTD

KONARK PUBLISHERS PVT LTD
206, First Floor, Peacock Lane,
Shahpur Jat,
New Delhi-110 049
Phone: +91-11-41055065, 65254972
Email: india@konarkpublishers.com
Website: www.konarkpublishers.com

Konark Publishers International
8615, 13th Ave SW,
Seattle WA 98106
Phone: (415) 409-9988
Email: us@konarkpublishers.com

First published 2018

Cataloging in Publication Data--DK
Courtesy: D.K. Agencies (P) Ltd. <docinfo@dkagencies.com>

Sreenivasan, T. P., author.
Education of an ambassador: reflections on higher education reform in Kerala/TP Sreenivasan.
pages cm
Includes index.
ISBN 9789322008895

1. Higher education and state—India—Kerala. 2. Educational change—India—Kerala. 3. Sreenivasan, T. P. I. Title.

LCC LA1154.K47S64 2018 | DDC 378.5483 23

Editor: Preeta Priyamvada

Typeset by The Laser Printers, New Delhi, and printed at Thomson Press (India) Ltd.

For Lekha,
who joined my journey of education
from my days as a teacher
in Mar Ivanios College, Thiruvananthapuram

CONTENTS

	Foreword by *NR Madhava Menon*	*ix*
	Introduction	*xv*
1.	Turning the Other Cheek	1
2.	An Act for Inaction	12
3.	Team without Team Spirit	20
4.	Unfinished Reform of the Semester System	25
5.	Reluctantly Autonomous	31
6.	State Assessment and Accreditation	37
7.	Teaching the Teachers	43
8.	Industry and Academia as Partners	48
9.	Fear of Privatisation	51
10.	A University for the Police	59
11.	RUSA in Ruins	63
12.	*Samaagati*: Gender Justice on Campus	68
13.	Arabic as an Asset	71
14.	A Policy for Higher Education	75
15.	Uniform Act for Universities	82

16. IT@Colleges 85

17. Incentives for Teachers 88

18. Liberalisation of Academic Travel 90

19. Research: The Right Way 93

20. *Higher Education for the Future*: A Journal for the Council 95

21. Clustering of Colleges 97

22. Cabbages and Kings 100

ANNEXURES 105

INDEX 240

FOREWORD

Higher education in the country, one can say, is drifting without proper direction under the changing political and economic environment at the Centre and in the States. The Yashpal Committee Report on Rejuvenation of Higher Education (2009) and the earlier Report submitted by the National Knowledge Commission (2005) gave certain policy guidelines for restructuring the system of higher education to support economic development while improving access, equity and quality at all levels. Following it, the then Central Government formulated a set of six legislative proposals and got them introduced in Parliament. Unfortunately, they could not be enacted and were allowed to lapse.

Meanwhile, the 12th Plan, which contained significant proposals for the education sector got the attention of the Government. States were persuaded uniformly to set up Higher Education Councils as independent authority to help plan development schemes and streamline educational administration directed towards autonomy, accountability and quality improvement in colleges and universities. With the introduction of the Rashtriya Uchchatar Shiksha Abhiyan, popularly known as RUSA, by the Central Government, the State Higher Education Council became more powerful in as much as central funding to

State universities and colleges got routed through the Council. However, in Kerala the Council (KSHEC) remained largely an advisory body with the Government wanting to maintain the status quo. The story of the function of the KSHEC under the stewardship of its Vice Chairman TP Sreenivasan during 2011–16 is contained in this volume. The author, a diplomat-turned educator, has a record of public service in different capacities combining administration with scholarship, rare among civil servants. The book makes interesting reading on how the system resists change despite changes being introduced from time to time!

Having been a product of higher education in Kerala in the 1950s and having been an educator and educational administrator outside Kerala for over 55 years, I am equally convinced as Sreenivasan that 'Kerala can realise its full potential only if fundamental changes are made in the mindset, outlook, work culture and ethics of its people' (Introduction, P-XV). The degree of bureaucratic control and the extent of political interference in higher education in Kerala are not only killing academic initiatives but posing potential risks to the career prospects of our graduates. Sreenivasan's book is a revealing document on what keeps higher education in Kerala regressive while talented youth migrate in large numbers to institutions outside the State for higher studies.

Kerala has the distinction of spending a sizeable chunk of its revenue on education and achieving total literacy which, in turn, has led to the betterment of the quality of life of its people. This was achieved with the participation of the private sector in a big way, and successive Governments encouraged the trend with the result that the majority of higher education institutions today are managed by civil society groups. Yet there is opposition to privatisation on ideological grounds and determined efforts are often made by some political parties to defeat every effort to reform standards in those institutions. Teachers, students and even the ministerial staff of colleges and universities are unionised on the basis of their political affiliations and organise strikes and violent protests disrupting the academic calendar and forcing students to private tuitions and self-study just to pass examinations. The result is unemployable graduates in large numbers who are good at nothing else but politics of the Kerala variety. A demonstration of this phenomenon is what Kerala saw in the ugly episode at the Global Education Meet at Trivandrum which the author explains in vivid detail in the very first chapter of the book.

The Scheme of the Kerala State Higher Education Council Act, 2007, as the author argues, is designed to limit its role to advisory and recommendatory functions, leaving it to the Department of Education of the Government to decide whether to act on it or to ignore without even putting it up for consideration of the authorities! It is no wonder, therefore, that most of the well-constructed Reports of the KSHEC on quality improvement in colleges and universities still remain buried in the department without any decision being made on them. I feel personally gratified that the Report of the Committee set up by the KSHEC on autonomy of colleges which I chaired got implemented despite an insensitive bureaucracy in place. What happened since then to autonomous colleges in the State is typical of the Kerala higher education establishment and is of too recent history to recall here.

The Council, in the four and a half years of its existence, did succeed to shake up institutional lethargy, gather a lot of information on academic performance of colleges and lack of accountability in them and proposed strategies to show them the path of academic excellence. RUSA was conceived to make Higher

Education Council the change agent to assist colleges and universities in the State to transform themselves as institutions of excellence. But the KSHEC itself lacked autonomy and was made an appendage of the Department of Education. As the author points out 'the Council and the Department worked in parallel tracks' which explains why most of the Reports of the Council did not receive the attention they deserved from the Government. However, compared to the work of the other State Councils, KSHEC in a short period, has left an impressive record in which one can find the architecture of a policy framework for higher education reforms potentially capable of redeeming lost ground in pursuit of quality improvement in higher education.

The author has strong words to describe the manipulative and self-serving strategies employed by officials to undermine the efficiency of the Council's functioning and on the matter of decision-making even at the highest levels of Government! It is a sad commentary on how petty politics and turf war among officials lead to bad governance and injury to public interest. Reading the experience of a celebrated administrator who worked as the Head of KSHEC, one wonders whether the higher education scenario in the State can expect any substantial reform in the near future.

With the change of Government, a one-man Committee recommended restructuring the Council itself which reportedly got approval of the Cabinet as well. Meanwhile, at the Central level there are Reports of new National Policy on Education in the offing. The budget speech of the Union Finance Minister spoke of 20 universities being selected, 10 from the public sector and 10 from the private sector, giving them full autonomy and funding support to transform themselves as world-class institutions. How these initiatives are going to be aligned with Kerala's ideology-driven, anti-privatisation and merit-neutral educational agenda is not clear. The idea of strengthening educational institutions in the public sector is a good policy, provided it leads to steady improvement in quality and standards. Otherwise, investment in higher education is a wastage of resources resulting in all-round mediocrity among the so-called educated class.

The book carries details of a series of changes introduced in the system responding to the demands of the times and directions from educational authorities. The 20 annexes included in the volume reflect the development of the thought processes of the author while being engaged in the challenging tasks entrusted to him by the State Government. They reveal the strength and weakness of the system and the frustrations a reformer might face in the Kerala context. They are to be read by all those who are involved in higher education if they desire to contribute to its improvement.

TP Sreenivasan is an asset for enlightened intellectual discourse in any society. I am glad that he continues to be involved in preparing Kerala youth who aspire to join the civil services. I hope, despite political differences, the Government in power will utilise his services for shaping a better society based on constitutional values and civic consciousness. I wish Sreenivasan many more years of active life and service to society, forgetting the pain that a certain misguided youth inflicted on him towards the end of his tenure in KSHEC.

NR Madhava Menon
Chancellor,
National University of Educational Planning and Administration, New Delhi
Honorary Director, Bar Council of Kerala
MK Nambyar Academy for Continuing Legal Education, Kochi

INTRODUCTION

Diplomats, even ambassadors, have to get educated continuously because of the frequency with which they move from city to city, country to country and continent to continent. They have to learn ways and means to deal with new issues, new cultures, new languages and new circumstances to function effectively. I, therefore, welcomed the opportunity to move from diplomacy to education as another challenge to learn to work in a new field. I was encouraged by the fact that many diplomats had turned educationists and vice versa.

My experience was an eye-opener to the higher education system in Kerala, the bureaucracy at different levels and the strengths and weaknesses of the State. It convinced me that Kerala can realise its full potential only if fundamental changes are made in the mindset, outlook, work culture and ethics of its people. It was education of an ambassador in the true sense of the word.

As the Vice Chairman of the Kerala State Higher Education Council (KSHEC) appointed by the Government in 2011, I was engaged in an effort to reform the higher education system in Kerala, with the involvement of some of the best experts in the field in Kerala and outside. In 16 Reports submitted to the Government, we laid out a roadmap for reform, touching upon the most crucial areas, such as infrastructure, teachers' training, technology-based education, autonomy, research and internationalisation.

The most significant achievement of the KSHEC during my time was the creation of awareness of the need to bring about major changes in education, leading to what I called 'Higher Education 2.0' that we proposed within six months of the formation of the Council. A beginning was made by the establishment of autonomous colleges, reforming of the semester system, introducing an India semester programme for foreign students, and organising training of teachers and administrative staff. Action was also initiated to set up a Kerala State Accreditation and Assessment Council and a Faculty Academy.

I believe that higher education has changed globally more in the last 10 years than in the previous 100 years. Unless we catch up with these changes and reform the way we teach and learn, we will be unable to prepare our younger generation to make use of the opportunities and meet the challenges of the 21st century. The demographic dividend we will have as the nation with the largest young workforce in the world will become meaningless unless we prepare youngsters for the professions of the 21st century. Most of the jobs being done around the world today will cease to exist in a few years on account of the growth of new technology. It is believed, for instance, that children born in 2017 will never see a driving licence!

It is unfortunate that most of our recommendations have remained unimplemented. The reasons for not implementing our recommendations are not far to seek. Proposals like allowing the operation of private universities in Kerala and cooperation with foreign universities were countered on ideological grounds. But many other reforms could have been implemented if only the Government, particularly the bureaucracy, had the necessary determination to bring about change. The Reports were not studied or processed for decisions by the Government on account of general lethargy and turf battles. The indifference to carefully crafted studies and recommendations was bewildering.

The purpose of this volume is to highlight the unfinished business of reform in higher education by explaining the logic of the measures recommended by the Council, the benefits that are likely to accrue to higher education if they are implemented and to stress the need for the recommendations to be examined by the Government.

As an advisory body, the KSHEC was at the mercy of the Department of Higher Education, which had its own priorities. The effort and the resources deployed by the Council will be fruitless if its recommendations, put together in this volume, are not examined and implemented to the extent possible.

We, as the members of the Executive Council, have the satisfaction that we have done our best to study the needs of higher education and suggested measures to transform the system. It is up to the Government to examine the roadmap we have provided and to move forward to modernise our higher education system. In a world which is embracing dramatic changes in the manner of teaching, learning and examining, we cannot afford to ignore the compulsions of change. Change will definitely come one day, but precious time will be lost at the cost of a whole generation of young people.

I delivered lectures, gave interviews and wrote columns on different aspects of higher education. Some of them have been reproduced in the Annexes to trace the evolution of my thinking as I learnt my lessons.

I would like to place on record my appreciation for the unfailing courtesies extended to me by the then Chief Minister, Oommen Chandy, and the Education Minister, Abdu Rabb. I also thank my colleagues in the Executive Council, the other experts and the supporting staff for their encouragement and cooperation.

I am grateful to NR Madhava Menon, Chancellor, National University of Educational Planning and Administration, New Delhi, Honorary Director, Bar Council of Kerala, MK Nambyar Academy for Continuing Legal Education, Kochi for reading the manuscript and writing a befitting Foreword for this book. I thank the other eminent educationists, Meenakshi Gopinath, Jules Tareen, Jancy James and G Gopakumar for adding words of appreciation. I am indebted to Divya Iyer for making valuable suggestions to improve the text. My appreciation also to the Publisher, KPR Nair and my Editor, Priyanka Sarkar for the efficient production of the book.

TP Sreenivasan
January 2018

Chapter 1

TURNING THE OTHER CHEEK

'*But I tell you, do not resist an evil person. If anyone slaps you on the right cheek, turn to them the other cheek also.*'

(Matthew 5:39 New Testament)

The morning broke on 29 January 2016, in a politically tense atmosphere in Kerala. The previous day, a vigilance court in Thrissur had ordered an investigation against Chief Minister Oommen Chandy in the light of the allegations that a femme fatale of Kerala politics, had raised before the Solar Commission. One of his Ministers had already resigned in similar circumstances a few days earlier. The air was thick with rumours that the Chief Minister might also resign that morning. The opposition launched a violent agitation early that morning to press the Chief Minister to resign. At the same time, it was expected that the Chief Minister would file an appeal in the High Court and he might get a reprieve if the High Court decided in his favour. In fact, a decision of the High Court lifted the cloud the same morning, leaving the opposition more frustrated.

To me the challenge that morning was to ensure that the Global Education Meet, scheduled to be inaugurated that morning by the Chief Minister, would proceed without any interruption. Nearly 200 international, national and state delegates had arrived and the atmosphere of tension in the city was of primary concern. I set off for the venue of the Meet, The Leela Hotel in Kovalam, with my wife fairly early and reached the entrance to the hotel. I was told later that the student demonstrators had declared that they would not allow the Chief Minister, the Education Minister and me to enter the venue to prevent the Meet from taking place. I had not even imagined that violence would be used to prevent an honest discussion on educational reform.

A crowd of about 200 youngsters was blocking the entrance to the hotel, but a police officer told me that I could walk through the crowd as several others had done a little earlier. As I walked into the crowd, someone identified me and announced that I should be stopped. As I walked back, I was mildly attacked from behind, but as I came out, someone, who accompanied me, as though to protect me, slapped me sharply on my right cheek, making me fall on the street. However, I felt that an unseen hand had saved me from injury and I was able to get up and walk with the help of a colleague who accompanied me. The police did nothing either to prevent the attack or to rescue me. I reached my car, joined my wife and drove to the home of our friends, Mathew and Sally, who lived close to the Leela Hotel. They were surprised to see us, but welcomed us with open arms as they always did. Several other participants of the Meet also took refuge in the same house. I managed to speak to the Home Minister, who promised immediate action and a police contingent arrived to remove the demonstrators. Within half an hour, the blockade was cleared and I was able to reach the venue and welcome the delegates. I apologised for the delay in commencing the Meet and said that when a section of students declared that they would block the Meet at any cost, I had not realised that they would go to the extent of resorting to violence. I characterised the incident as 'militant democracy in action.' The Meet went like clockwork afterwards, though the incidents of the morning cast a shadow over it. The discussions were lively and rich, the atmosphere was congenial and the arrangements were impeccable. The Kovalam Declaration encapsulated the outcome and showed the way forward.

I realised the seriousness of the incident and its impact on the public only when I watched its news coverage and the wide protests it triggered around the state. I did not have to explain anything, as every detail was clear, particularly that I was unprovoked even in the face of insult and violence. The condemnation of the incident and regret over such intolerance on discussing issues was very strong. There was unanimous disapproval of the method used to counter the measures to revamp higher education. The media gave wide coverage to the incident and speculated as to how the politics of violence was emerging as a threat to democracy when the elections were approaching. The leadership withdrew some of the allegations it had made personally against me such as my being a foreign agent of privatisation.

I was overwhelmed by the sympathy and support that the incident engendered across the entire spectrum of public opinion. Several leading newspapers not only reported every aspect of the incident, but also condemned it in no uncertain terms. Several dailies wrote editorials, pointing out the dangers of intolerance of consideration of ideas and the cult of violence. Many saw the incident as symptomatic of a new cult of violence, which would be the order of the day if the Leftists came to power. The largest and the most respected newspaper, *Malayala Manorama* carried an editorial on 30 January 2016, entitled 'A slap on the cheek of literate Kerala—Attack on TP Sreenivasan condemned.' It said 'The attack by SFI activists on TP Sreenivasan, who has brought us pride by holding aloft the names of Kerala and India nationally and internationally, is a slap on the face of Kerala, which prides itself in its literacy and cultural heritage.'

Rajeev Srinivasan, a reputed intellectual and writer, wrote in his Rediff column:

> ...the incident in which retired ambassador TP Sreenivasan was slapped so hard that he fell down was truly shocking, even to those used to the antics of Leftists. As a respected and prominent citizen of Thiruvananthapuram, the ambassador is an active participant in many fora, as the head of the Kerala Higher Education Council, as well as a Rediff columnist and a host of the foreign affairs television programme, Videsha Vicharam. He is an urbane diplomat who represented India's interests in many countries, and the assault on him is in a way an assault on the Indian State as well. Why would the Communists (the Student Federation of India) do this? I have three possible answers: One, they are specifically opposed to the Global Education Meet that the ambassador organised. Two, they are beginning to realise their days are numbered in Kerala. Three, the standard modus operandi of Leftists is anarchism because they are not constrained by any codes of ethics. Roughly, the bad, the good, and the ugly.

The following highly supportive and sensitive report appeared on Rediff.com on 1 February 2016:

> TP Sreenivasan, who was manhandled by the Students' Federation of India (SFI) activists before the inauguration session of the Global Education Meet in Thiruvananthapuram on Friday, did not let the incident affect him or the prestigious Meet. He proceeded to deliver his welcome address, with just a passing mention of what had happened, his wry sense of humour intact. 'I should apologise for the delay in convening the Inaugural Session of the Global Education Meet. As you have been informed, a section of students made an effort to block entry to the Convention Centre to protest against what they call "commercialisation of higher education",' he said.

He added: 'Although we had explained the goals of the Meet, also through my op-eds in two leading dailies, *The Times of India* and *Mathrubhumi*, the SFI had declared that they would stop the meet at "any cost". I did not realise that the cost was an attack on me, but I am happy to survive it to be here to welcome you. I am sure that our friends from abroad will see it as "militant democracy" in operation.' With Chief Minister Oommen Chandy giving the Meet a miss, it was left to Prof. William Tierney to inaugurate the Meet.

'The Global Education Meet,' Ambassador Sreenivasan said, 'was the culmination of a journey my colleagues in the Kerala State Higher Education Council and I began in October 2011. We set an agenda for ourselves to create a Higher Education 2.0 with special attention to infrastructure, teachers' training, technology-based learning, autonomy, research and internationalisation. Although the progress on the ground has been modest, we are leaving behind a treasure of recommendations, painstakingly prepared with the participation of some of the best academics in the country.

They contain a roadmap, a way forward, which, if implemented, will transform higher education in Kerala. I am grateful to the Government for entrusting this task to us and for accepting our advice wherever feasible. I hope that we will have the mindset and the money one day to redefine higher education in Kerala. But as the attack by SFI activists shows, it is not going to be an easy task.'

But unfazed, this is what the Ambassador had to say about the SFI's fears of 'commercialisation of education': 'Over the centuries, we have welcomed and absorbed the best in many civilisations without being swept away by them. We should not be afraid to learn from others for fear of being overwhelmed by globalisation. The message that has come from the World Economic Summit a few days ago was that we are at the beginning of the fourth industrial revolution in the world and we cannot be part of it unless we join the education revolution, which is already under

> way. At the Meet, we are following the sage advice given by the great nationalist, Swami Vivekananda.
>
> "Stand on your own feet, and assimilate what you can, learn from every nation, take what is of use to you",' he said.
>
> 'Education has been a window to the world for India for years. But today, it is an absolute necessity, because India cannot play its legitimate role in global affairs without a higher education system, which matches the best in the world. We should not only innovate constantly but also emulate the best practices in the world and not insist on reinventing the wheel. Fears of commercialisation should not deter us from moving with the times.' Now, if only the hotheads in SFI paused to reflect on what Ambassador Sreenivasan said.

A concrete expression of solidarity came in the form of the monthly hoarding on top of the Kerala Travels building, which devoted its February hoarding to the attack on me. On an earlier occasion, when some political workers attacked an IAS officer, the hoarding had expressed pain and shame over the incident. This time, the hoarding had a picture of me with the inscription, 'A slap on the Sree of Kerala. We are again in pain and shame. *Sabko sanmati de bhagwan* (may God bless all with wisdom)!' The same hoarding appeared in different parts of the city subsequently. Other flex boards showed me on the road after the attack and blamed the Leftists for the cult of violence. It remained an election issue on Congress and BJP platforms. There were suggestions that I should cash in on the sympathy by contesting elections to the Legislative Assembly, but I successfully resisted them.

The Kerala High Court took a serious view of the attack on me. Justice Sunil Thomas, while refusing bail to the accused, observed that slapping me should be considered more serious than any other person being attacked and it was 'an affront to the society and shocked social consciousness.' The Lokayukta of Kerala registered a case on his own against my assailants.

More shocking than the behaviour of the students was the attitude of the police personnel present at the venue. They could have easily prevented the incident by taking the necessary precautions, having advised me to walk through the demonstrators. But even worse, they did not come to my rescue even after I fell on the ground. This was attributed to general apathy and also the fear that they would be victimised if there was a change of Government after the elections. But it was heartwarming that the police realised their mistake and formally apologised to me in their house magazine and also at their annual function to which I was invited as the chief guest. The Police Chief took action against the men on duty and stated that more severe punishment should have been given to them.

The Chief Minister, the Education Minister and the Chief Secretary were among the hundreds of people who came home to express sympathy and solidarity. Twenty civic organisations in Thiruvananthapuram held a protest meeting on the day of the incident. Messages poured in from around the Globe. In an exceptional demonstration of solidarity, many Indians abroad organised a massive conference call to express sympathy and support. Many meetings were held by people of different hues to protest the onslaught. The BJP organised a well-attended event at the Martyrs' Memorial to condemn the incident, to which the leading intellectuals of Kerala were invited.

Many Leftist leaders expressed regret, sympathy and even condemnation of the incident. But the 'most unkindest cut of all' came from the then General Secretary of the Marxist Party. He said, 'First, he is not an educationist. Sreenivasan has served as an ambassador and he is an expert in that field. He was appointed as a special ambassador to privatise higher education. Academic City is not suitable for Kerala and we cannot accept the Academic City. United Democratic Front (UDF) leaders should ensure that our educationists do not become agents of foreign institutions'. The next day, he was reported to have said that his previous comment was without knowing the details and expressed regret. If he reads this book, it will be clear to him that the Council did much more than recommending private universities. The idea of the Academic City had emanated from the Department of Education.

In the midst of widespread sympathy and appreciation of the way I responded, a lone journalist tried to spread a canard that I had used abusive language against the students at some stage. But those who had seen the video had no doubt that I was polite and pleasant throughout. The journalist then went on to say that I had used a false designation in Vienna till I sent him a copy of my credentials document. He even alleged that I had closed down my website. Human depravity is boundless.

I have, doubtless, championed not only private investment in higher education, but also collaboration with foreign universities and autonomy. But these were part of a new 'Higher Education 2.0,' which had several proposals to improve the quality of state institutions. Those who wanted to deny the credit of higher education reform to the UDF Government used the internationalisation agenda to demonise the Global Meet as a conspiracy to smuggle in private universities and foreign universities. A number of former Vice-Chancellors, who had not succeeded in increasing the quality of higher education during their time, spread the theory that the reform proposals were dangerous to the education system. They did not have an alternative plan to increase quality, but condemned every move of the Government as misguided and motivated. As the champion of change and the most visible spokesperson of the Government on higher education, I became the target of the opposition, which resulted in the Kovalam incident.

The irony of it was that all the controversies that surrounded the Global Education Meet were created by others. Take for instance, the name, Global Education Meet, which was a red rag for some because of its link with globalisation. When I organised a similar conference in 2014, I called it an International Conference on Transnational Education and there was no objection to the concept. A proposal to hold another Conference to follow up the Thiruvananthapuram Declaration in 2015 was shot down by the political masters and I was told that there would be a Global Education Meet (GEM). Nothing was known to me till November 2015, when I was told that it was decided that the Department of Higher Education, the Higher Education Council and the Federation of Indian Chambers of Commerce and Industry (FICCI) would jointly hold the GEM in January 2016. I pointed out that time was short and that there was no role for FICCI in the substance of the Meet. But an understanding had already been reached to involve FICCI in the Meet by paying a hefty fee. The involvement of FICCI was a major point of contention about the Meet.

The inclusion in the GEM agenda of the International Higher Education Zones and an Academic City also came as a surprise, because I had always maintained that the kind of Academic City that the Minister saw and a team studied and recommended would not work unless foreign universities and private universities were permitted to operate in the state. The whole thing was conceived on the assumption that self-financing institutions with foreign linkages would operate from the Academic City with affiliation to existing universities in Kerala. I continuously expressed reservations, but bids were invited from private individuals to establish institutions in the Academic City and International Higher Education Zones. These ideas were included on the understanding that the Meet could discuss their feasibility and the Government could benefit from the discussion in giving final shape to the authority envisaged to run these entities. As anticipated, most delegates made the point that affiliated institutions would not be forthcoming and that private universities and foreign universities should be permitted, if the Academic City and Zones were to work.

Although I inherited a number of decisions taken by others, I decided to make a success of the GEM, essentially to highlight the need for change. As the Vice Chairman of the Organising Committee, I had to reconcile the differences between the 3 entities involved. Compared to the earlier conference that the Council handled by itself, the GEM was harder, but there were no major hurdles. My insistence on avoiding ostentation and pomp was resented by some, but its intrinsic merit was recognised. Publicity was considered unnecessary as the Meet was open only to invitees. Arches, flex boards and souvenirs were avoided and the savings were used to gift quality bags to the delegates. The total cost estimated initially was reduced to half because of the austerity measures imposed.

The substantive preparations for the GEM were done by a competent and thoughtful group under my supervision. The Theme Paper outlined every aspect of the Meet, leaving no room for ambiguity or misinterpretation. The objectives of the Meet and the agenda for the future were spelt out in great detail. Even the worst critics of the exercise had nothing to say against it and it was widely used in the discussions. The draft Kovalam Declaration, which was prepared with meticulous care, was approved by consensus with minor changes.

The imperative for change in the education system came out loud and clear after the GEM. The work of the State Higher Education Council came to light and the public support for its initiatives increased. The fact that the children of several political leaders were getting educated abroad even when they opposed any collaboration with the same institutions shocked the common man. They paid a price for the thoughtless action of the students at a critical time for them.

As for myself, what mattered was that I escaped injury and managed to proceed with the Meet. But the regret is that the incident has caused a setback to the reform process. Those who came to the Meet saw for themselves that Kerala was not yet ready to change with the times and they lost interest in the projects that they had proposed. Tears must be shed for our younger generation, which is falling victim to political machinations.

I turned my other cheek to my attackers as they knew not what they were doing to themselves. But the tragedy is that I had to do that at every step of the journey in pursuit of reform in higher education. The very authorities who entrusted me with the responsibility of running the system lacked energy and enthusiasm and were concerned only about protecting their own interests. They had no hesitation in countering new ideas, delaying action and conspiring against change. The saga of reform in higher education was a saga of constant resistance and manipulation and my having to show the other cheek all the time.

Chapter 2

AN ACT FOR INACTION

The Kerala State Higher Education Council (KSHEC) was created by an Act of the Kerala Legislature in 2007, as advised by the University Grants Commission (UGC) 'to occupy an operational space in between the Government and universities and between universities and apex-level regulatory bodies, with the objectives of (i) ensuring the autonomy and accountability of all institutions of higher learning in the state, (ii) promoting academic excellence and social justice by providing academic input to the State Government for policy formulation and perspective planning, and (iii) guiding the growth of higher education in accordance with the socio-economic requirements of the state.'

With these objects in view, the Council has the following responsibilities:

- Render advice to the Government, universities and other institutions of higher education in the state.
- Coordinate the roles of the Government, universities and apex regulatory agencies in higher education within the state.
- Evolve new concepts and programmes in higher education.

- Provide common facilities in higher education without impinging upon the autonomy of other institutions of higher education.

Possible actions to be undertaken by the Council are:

- Provide academic input to the Government and to the universities, research institutions and other centres of higher education in the State for the formulation and implementation of the policies on higher education and evolve a perspective plan for the development of higher education, suo moto or on the suggestion from Government or requests from universities or other institutions.
- Undertake independent research for the generation of new ideas for the promotion of social justice and academic excellence in higher education, hold awareness programmes for the academia and initiate or propose or pilot projects on an experimental basis in selected higher education institutions for implementation of the new ideas.
- Undertake human resources development planning for the State and plan the growth and development of higher education in accordance with such planning.
- Evolve guidelines for linkages of an academic nature between higher education institutions in the State and institutions within and outside the country.
- Evolve programmes in order to promote the relevance of higher education for the economic, social and cultural development of the State.
- Review existing guidelines and furnish recommendations for regulating admissions to various courses and for appointments to the posts of teachers and teacher-administrators in universities, colleges and other institutions of higher education.

- Suggest improvements in curriculum and syllabi in accordance with the changing societal and academic requirements and facilitate the development and publication of appropriate teaching material, including textbooks, educational software and e-learning facilities in order to improve the quality of education.
- Organise short-term courses to train and update the knowledge and skills of higher education teaching personnel, educational administrators and other similarly situated.
- Advise the Government on the starting of new courses, colleges, and other higher education institutions in the State.
- Make proposals for the generation and utilisation of funds in accordance with the objectives of this Act.
- Evolve general guidelines for the release of grants by the Government to universities and other institutions of higher education and to advise the Government about the release of such grants to each university and other institutions of higher education.
- Evolve schemes for providing equitable opportunities for higher education and scholarships, freeships and financial assistance to underprivileged students and coordinate the implementation of the welfare programmes of the Central and the State Governments, and other Central and State-level funding agencies for the Scheduled Castes and Scheduled Tribes and other eligible backward classes.
- Review periodically the Statutes, Ordinances and Regulations of the universities in the State and suggest appropriate improvements for the realisation of the objectives of social justice and academic excellence in

education and suggest the framework for new Statutes, Ordinances, or Regulations for existing universities or other institutions of higher education or new universities or other institutions of higher education.

- Provide common facilities for the entire state by establishing centres, namely:
  - (i) Centre for Research on Policies in Higher Education;
  - (ii) Curriculum Development Centre;
  - (iii) Centre for Capacity Building in respect of faculty and educational administrators;
  - (iv) State Council for Assessment of Higher Education Institutions;
  - (v) Examination Reforms Cell;
  - (vi) Human Resources Development, Employment and Global Skills Development Cell.
- Hold discussions, and conduct workshops and seminars with the objective of facilitating the widest possible consultations with experts and stakeholders including organisations of students and teachers for formulating the policies on higher education and facilitating their proper implementation.
- Facilitate the development of a synergic relationship among different agencies such as the State Government, universities, colleges and other institutions of higher education in the State and the Central Government and regulatory bodies at the national level.
- Co-ordinate various programmes being promoted and undertaken by Central and State Governments and national-level bodies such as the University Grants Commission, All India Council for Technical Education,

National Council for Teacher Education, Medical Council of India, Bar Council of India and other similar statutory bodies and State-level institutions like universities, research institutions, colleges and other institutions of higher education in the territory of India.

- Provide a forum for interaction among the academy, industries, agriculture and service sectors.
- Facilitate the conducting of workshops and seminars on questions of importance in higher education in different parts of the State.
- Undertake necessary steps for establishing inter-linkages between research and learning processes.
- Promote extension activities in colleges, institutions and universities and encourage their integration into the curriculum so that the students and teachers become sensitive to social issues.
- Promote sports and cultural activities in the colleges, other institutions and universities and integrate them with the co-curricular activities.
- Perform such other functions for the realisation of the twin objectives of social justice and excellence in higher education.
- Suggest steps for promoting democratisation and academic autonomy of universities and other institutions of higher education.
- Evolve schemes to sensitise the students to environmental and gender issues.

While the objectives are laudable, the responsibilities and functions of the Council are only research-oriented. The Council is free to study any aspect of higher education in any institution and make recommendations to the institutions and the Government. It is expected to coordinate the roles of the Government, universities and apex regulatory agencies in higher education. But there is no mechanism by which the Council is able to follow the activities of the institutions in a routine manner. The Council can seek information, but responses are few and far between. No advice is sought from the Council on specific issues. Consequently, the Council works on the sidelines on issues that may have no relevance to the work of the higher education institutions.

The methodology adopted by the Council is to pick and choose issues for study with the help of experts and prepare reports for submission to the Government. The reports thus submitted are filed away in the Higher Education Department as the Department has no set procedure for examining the reports and submitting them for consideration at the political level. Neither the UGC nor the Ministry of Human Resource Development sends any communication to the Council, and the Department has no obligation to seek the advice of the Council on matters of policy. Some complicated issues of procedure are sent to the Council merely for the sake of form to avoid taking an administrative decision.

The Act provides for the establishment of six centres, including a State Council for Assessment of Higher Education Institutions, but no resources or personnel have been provided. The activities are undertaken by three research officers without any supporting staff. The only activity the Council can undertake on its own is training of teachers through short courses.

The Governor of Kerala is the Patron of the Council by virtue of his office. The Chief Minister is the visitor and the Chairman is the Minister for Education. The Vice Chairman is the Executive Head of the Council and the Member Secretary is responsible for the coordination of the academic functions of the Council. The administration of the Council is handled by the Registrar.

The Council has a three-tier structure with the Chief Minister as the Chairman of an Advisory Council, the Minister for Education as the Chairman of the Governing Council and the Vice Chairman as the Chairman of the Executive Council. But, in practice, only the Executive Council functioned. The Advisory Council was never formed and the Governing Council was formed only three years after the Executive Council was formed, despite the fact that I had made suggestions about the composition of these bodies and kept reminding the Principal Secretary, Higher Education, the Minister of Education and the Chief Minister. I had pointed out that the KSHEC would not be complete without the formation of the Governing Council and the Advisory Council.

The Executive Council has, apart from the Vice Chairman and the Member Secretary, seven other members, including five educationists, one of the Vice Chancellors and the Secretary, Higher Education. The Executive Council reports to the Governing Council, particularly on the audited accounts, handled by the Executive Council. The term of the Council is for four years, extendable for six months. The Vice Chairman has the status, salary and perks of a Vice Chancellor and the Member Secretary has those of a Pro-Vice Chancellor.

The Council is considered an autonomous body, but the Act does not confer such a status on the Council and it has no authority to take any action on its own. Framing of regulations and other administrative actions need the prior approval of the Government. The Council has been designed as a sinecure with no expectation of any action. The Department of Higher Education and the universities consider it a distraction rather than a vital part of the decision-making process in higher education. The tardy implementation of the reports of the Council was not on account of opposition from outside, but from the enemies within.

Chapter 3

TEAM WITHOUT TEAM SPIRIT

My appointment as the Vice Chairman of the KSHEC was a complete surprise to me. Chief Minister Oommen Chandy and KPCC President Ramesh Chennithala and some others had sounded me about the possibility of my services being used by the new United Democratic Front (UDF) Government. However, I thought that it would be either to help with the overseas Keralites or with investment promotion, the two areas in which I had relevant experience. My immediate reaction to the offer of the Council was that I would not qualify, as I was not an educationist or a former Vice Chancellor. Having seen some brilliant Vice Chancellors in the University of Kerala, such as Samuel Mathai, I had nursed a secret desire to be the Vice Chancellor of Kerala University someday, though I never disclosed it to anyone. I was also aware that many distinguished persons had shone as both diplomats and educationists such as Sardar KM Panikkar, MC Chagla, Nurul Hassan and Hamid Ansari. It was pointed out to me that my exposure to the world and familiarity with higher education in some advanced countries might be helpful in reforming our system. I was, therefore, delighted that I had the opportunity to make a contribution to higher education in Kerala. I was completely unaware that the post of the Vice Chairman was a sinecure with no role in the implementation of reforms. Moreover, I had not expected that the Department of Higher Education would undermine it for no obvious reasons.

I discovered that the members of the Council were selected on political and caste considerations. Each could be identified with a party and a caste. The Member Secretary and five educationists, who were nominated to the Council, were clearly representing different interests. The Member Secretary told me on day one that his loyalty would be to his party and the Minister and not to me. This turned out to be a great impediment in the work of the Council throughout and marked the biggest challenge to the smooth functioning of the Council. Groups were created within the Council and the office and decisions were overturned by manipulating the system. I needed all my diplomatic skills, patience and persuasion to ensure that the work of the Council did not suffer on account of the rifts within.

The other members of the Council were part-time members and they were constructive and supportive of most of the ideas suggested by me. Initially, there was a tendency to bring in the familiar rift between the Vice Chancellors and the Syndicates into the Council, but since we worked in the realm of concepts and ideas and not administrative or personnel matters, the Council managed to work harmoniously. Most of the ideas I brought before the Council either personally or through the various expert groups were accepted by them, as long as they had a role to play. It was the form rather than substance that mattered to them and I took care to maintain their visibility in the various projects undertaken by the Council. The academic experience of some of the members was very valuable to me.

The Vice Chancellors of the major universities in Kerala served on the Council for one year each. Their involvement was minimal because of their own preoccupations, but they had much to contribute to the discussions in the Council. The Secretary of the Higher Education Department was an ex-officio member of the Executive Council, but he rarely attended the meetings and did not care much about the work of the Council, except when he wanted to use the Council to promote some of his own ideas. By and large, the Council and the Department worked in parallel tracks. The Department picked and chose our recommendations when it suited them and ignored others as disruptive or impractical. The advent of the Rashtriya Uchchatar Shiksha Abhiyan (RUSA), which involved sharing of financial and planning responsibilities with the Council, aggravated the situation further.

The Council Secretariat consisted of three academics as Research Officers, some persons on deputation from the State Government and others on contract from the market. Some of the academics were good and worked well, but some others turned out to be misfits in an administrative set-up and quickly resorted to manipulation and self-seeking manoeuvre. As for the junior bureaucracy, there was much to be desired in terms of punctuality, loyalty and dedication. Evading responsibility on one pretext or another appeared to be a common problem, though some of them worked hard and made a mark. The contract employees worked better because their continuance depended on satisfactory performance. The junior bureaucracy I worked with in the Ministry of External Affairs and our missions abroad generally shone in comparison with its counterpart in Kerala.

The methodology I adopted in the Council was to examine the work done by the previous council with a view to completing it and rectifying the problems encountered. A mix of the old agenda and the new agenda was presented to the Council as soon as we took over and the Council decided to design a 'Higher Education 2.0' to suit the needs of the new century. A blueprint for action was placed before a National Seminar in June 2012, which approved it without dissent. We identified infrastructure, training of teachers, technology-based teaching and learning, autonomy, research and internationalisation as the areas, which deserved immediate attention. (The Theme Paper of the Seminar is in Annex 19.) Thereafter, we proceeded to set up expert groups to study the measures necessary to reform higher education. We submitted 16 Reports to the Government, some of which were implemented. The recommendations constituted a comprehensive plan, which had to be examined by the Government and implemented as a whole. Instead, the Department of Higher Education treated it like a menu card, from which they picked up items that suited their taste, purse and political expediency. As a result, the work of the Council remained on paper, without a decisive impact on the higher education scene.

The Council can, however, claim credit for carrying the message for the need for change in all sectors of higher education. My colleagues and I travelled the length and breadth of the State and used every opportunity to stress the need for higher education to catch up with the changes taking place in the rest of India and abroad. There was wide acceptance of the ideas in principle, but stiff resistance at the practical level left the system largely untouched.

The politicisation of higher education at every level took me by complete surprise. This was so with regard to appointments at all levels. The system was devised in such a way that interaction between the Government and the Opposition was totally excluded. None from the Opposition parties or the academics, who served the previous Government was involved in the Council or in its subsidiary bodies. The Government gave me no such instruction, but the Council was adamant that anyone associated with the previous Government should be kept out of any of the Committees. This principle had the blessings at the political and the department levels. Part of the reason for this was the existence of rival unions to which the stakeholders belonged. They jealously guarded the system when their Government came to power on the plea that they were excluded in the previous dispensation. This complete division is at the heart of the misunderstanding about new policies and programmes. Without bipartisan support and a consensus, no reform of education is possible. The differences are not so far apart in substance. Even on the role of the private sector and foreign universities, there is enough agreement to fashion a common policy and strategy. Apart from being divided, the Council team remained alienated from other approaches and views.

Chapter 4

UNFINISHED REFORM OF THE SEMESTER SYSTEM

The first issue that faced the Council soon after its formation was the demand to abolish the Choice-Based Credit and Semester System (CBCSS) introduced by the previous Council. The logic was simply that the reform brought about in the system by the Left Democratic Front (LDF) should be reversed by the UDF. Many real and imaginary problems that cropped up on account of the introduction of the new system were brought up by sections of the teachers and students, and some members of the Council began to pressurise me to bring back the annual system. I took the view that the semester system had its merits and it should be preserved to remain modern and relevant. I agreed, however, to study the operation of the new system and to reform it further, if necessary.

I turned to my favourite teacher at the university college during the 1960s and a reputed educationist, Hridayakumari, to head a Committee to study the various issues that had come up in the working of the CBCSS in colleges affiliated to the universities in the State, and make recommendations for the improvement of the system. I also suggested that it should consider a common name for the new system, unification of syllabi in all the universities following the system, a common pattern of question papers and grading system, uniformity in the examination pattern and award of grades for semesters, and uniform distribution of marks to internal and external semester examinations.

The Committee collected views and suggestions from a large number of teachers, students and experts in education, including Vice Chancellors and Pro-Vice Chancellors, officials, political activists, intellectuals and various other members of the public. Representations from teachers and teachers' organisations form a greater chunk of the documents received. In addition to the formal meetings of the Committee, there were informal meetings of the Committee members with the Chairperson. Many teachers also took the trouble to meet the Chairperson, sometimes to present their problems, and sometimes to clarify some details of how the system worked.

Representatives of various teachers' organisations, non-teaching staff from the universities and affiliated colleges, students, parallel college associations, parents and public, experts of print and visual media and other individuals attended the sittings and submitted and shared their responses, apprehensions, suggestions and complaints. Apart from this, a large number of representations and memorandums were received by the Committee. Different agencies and organisations submitted detailed reports about the working of the system on the basis of surveys and interviews conducted among the students and teaching community and with other stakeholders. The Chairperson of the Committee received feedbacks, proposals and suggestions from the academia of the state, ranging over former and current Vice Chancellors and

Pro-Vice Chancellors, Controllers of Examinations, members of Boards of Studies, retired teachers, intellectuals, social and political activists, student and youth leaders, bureaucrats, etc. through her personal interaction with them.

After a painstaking review of the entire scenario, the Committee recommended that CBCSS be maintained, particularly for the following reasons:

- The UGC, the National Accreditation Council and certain other National bodies are strongly in favour of the new system. Any deviation from a National Policy or trend may create serious problems for the universities and the State Government, unless they are willing to take a pitched stand for the autonomy of universities.
- The old system was lacking in innovativeness and in the capacity to come to grips with fast-changing global conditions. It seemed as though the old system lost somewhere on its way the potential it may have had for self-criticism and self-renewal. It is in this context that this Committee opted for the CBCSS, hoping that the problems pointed out by it and the solutions suggested would be given serious consideration.

The Council formulated the following recommendations on the basis of the Hridayakumari Report:

1. Instead of grading, mark system should be introduced for each question. However, notional grading on the basis of marks should be indicated for each semester. Overall gradation should be on a 7-point scale and should be awarded only at the end of the programme.
2. For internal assessment of all courses, at the end of each semester, 10 marks should be awarded for test paper,

5 marks for seminar or assignment and 5 for attendance, with a total of 20 marks.

3. For external assessment, universities should conduct examinations for core subjects and compulsory language papers to be centrally evaluated at the end of the second, fourth and sixth semesters. All practical examinations should also be conducted at the end of the second, fourth and sixth semesters.
4. Examinations for the complementary subjects, electives, open courses and additional languages, should be conducted at the end of all semesters. All question papers should be set by the universities. The odd semester examination answer sheets should be evaluated by home evaluation and the even semester examination sheets should be evaluated by centralised evaluation.
5. In addition to semester breaks for students (maximum 10 days), there should be two months summer vacation.
6. A maximum of four credits may be awarded per semester to those who are actively engaged in co-curricular, extra-curricular activities, such as NCC, NSS, sports and arts.
7. Universities should make provisions for transfer of credits for those who take an inter-university or intra-university transfer, provided the student has a minimum of 20 credits in the credit bank.
8. No moderation should be awarded in any examination under CBCSS.
9. For informatics courses, qualified teachers and appropriate laboratories should be provided.
10. Methodology course should be shifted from UG to PG.
11. The Boards of Studies should rationalise and restructure the number of courses, syllabi and prescription of textbooks in order to make the semester system effective.

12. Boards of Studies should make the changes in the syllabi and textbooks in consultation with the teachers. At least two meetings of teachers may be held in every Department in every college, one in mid-year and one towards the year end. The recommendations of these meetings should be considered by the Boards of Studies.
13. The Boards of Studies should make sure that there is no political bias in textbooks, particularly propagandist literature.
14. As the language of higher education, English should receive extra attention. Graduates should be proficient in written and spoken English. Necessary changes may be made in the Curriculum by the Boards of Studies.
15. Boards of Studies have to be constantly in touch with renowned Indian universities, and at least a few foreign universities. Subject experts have to be identified in all major fields of study and endeavour, and consulted frequently. A format for the working of Boards of Studies could be devised so that structured work is possible.

The recommendations were accepted by the Government, but there was an uproar when they were presented to a group of selected stakeholders. Instead of examining the merits of the recommendations, many of them walked out on the plea that they were not consulted. It was obvious that the recommendations would not be fully implemented by the universities.

The universities were provided funding to hold workshops, etc. to explain the changes and to make optimum use of the reform measures, but the reforms were not fully implemented for various reasons. The recommendations relating to the constitution of the Boards of Studies and revision of syllabi and prescribed textbooks have remained largely unimplemented. Many teachers and students still remain unhappy with the semester system, mainly because of the extra work it imposes on them. Another effort should be made by the Council to review the system to bring uniformity in all the universities.

Chapter 5

RELUCTANTLY AUTONOMOUS

The blueprint for reform presented in the National Seminar in 2012 had stressed the need for greater autonomy to the universities and colleges. Following this, the Council mooted the idea of introducing autonomous colleges for the first time in Kerala. After initial resistance at the ministerial level, the Government encouraged us to do a study on the feasibility of the idea and a committee was constituted for the purpose with NR Madhava Menon in the chair. From outside the state, Meenakshi Gopinath and Jasintha Quadras joined the Committee.

The Committee studied the feasibility of autonomous colleges in Kerala in great detail by discussing it with a wide spectrum of scholars, administrators, students and the public. The Committee visited a successful autonomous college in Chennai and studied its functioning. The Committee was very impressed with the way new courses were introduced, the speed with which examination results were announced and the general atmosphere of efficiency and academic excellence. One of the popular courses introduced by the college was for a degree in fine arts. Having heard all the positive points about autonomy, the Committee asked the faculty members if there were any negative points. After much deliberation, we were told that the only negative point was that the teachers had to work really hard. This was obvious to us from the beginning as we observed that the teachers were devoting much time to administer autonomy.

The Committee observed that Quality is as important as Access and Equity in higher education because it is intended to enable its recipients to live a life of dignity while contributing to the development of society. Ever since Independence, there has been several attempts on the part of Central and State Governments, UGC, All India Council for Technical Education (AICTE) and similar regulatory bodies as well as universities and colleges to improve the quality of instruction offered. Nonetheless, because of heavy demand for access and consequent expansion of colleges and universities together with constraints on resources, standards of education could not cope up with expansion. The affiliating system, which played a useful role in managing access in the past occupied disproportionate time on administration of the system and undermined the capacities of universities and colleges to work towards research and development. Even curricular reform took a back seat in many universities. While there is no alternative in the present context to the system of affiliation, there is a need to seek fresh strategies for innovation and experimentation in the entire range of higher education activities at the institutional level. Acknowledging this need, the UGC evolved in 2007 a set of guidelines for autonomous colleges and encouraged the States and universities to give autonomy to at least 10 per cent of its colleges. There is enough evidence to show that autonomy leads to enhancement of academic standards and promotes student-centric learning in higher education.

Admittedly, there are colleges in Kerala in the Government sector as well as the private sector that deserve autonomy and can realise their full academic potential. The Committee, therefore, strongly recommended that Kerala should introduce this reform without further delay. The Committee welcomed the policy announcement in this regard in the 2013 Budget Speech of the Finance Minister and hoped that the recommendations will facilitate the grant of autonomy to deserving colleges in the State.

The Committee noted that there are many misgivings and apprehensions amply demonstrated in the Committee's interactions with stakeholders about what autonomy implies to colleges, universities, the State Government and the student body. The UGC Guidelines for autonomous colleges is very clear in this regard. Essentially, it is autonomy in respect of academic affairs, as this is how it is in places where quality matters. How should the curriculum be developed and the courses of study organised? How can the examination system be improved to make it a true measure of learning? What innovations need to be introduced in pedagogy using modern tools of technology in order to make learning student-centric? How can the academic calendar be developed to increase working days and to maximise learning opportunities for students? What extension activities and outreach programmes can enrich the curriculum while engaging the colleges with the communities where they are located? These questions and related measures may bring greater opportunities to teachers and staff of autonomous colleges.

To be able to do this and more on the academic front, colleges may need some degree of administrative autonomy. That is why the UGC Guidelines prescribe a new internal governance structure in place of the existing management. Thus, the Guidelines speak of a governing body for the college with 12 members in which existing management can nominate as many as 9 members including the Principal. The UGC, the State Government and the university to which the college is affiliated will have one nominee each in the governing body.

Each autonomous college will have its own Academic Council with four experts from outside the college nominated by the Governing Body and three nominees of the university. The Principal and all Heads of Departments of the college as well as four other teachers of the college are its members. The decisions of the College Academic Council do not need any ratification by the university. The college will have a Board of Studies attached to each Department to prepare the syllabi, teaching methods, examination, research and related academic activities. The Head of the Department is the Chairman of the Board of Studies. In short, autonomy does not rest with the management or the Principals of the colleges. It percolates down to every department and to every teacher, allowing space for innovation and creativity for the benefit of students at all levels.

Autonomy is to be sought and deserved. It is a voluntary process of the college concerned. On the basis of records and inspection, the UGC grants autonomy for an initial period of six years during which it sends teams to review functioning at periodic intervals. In other words, it is a carefully crafted, properly supervised and responsibly administered process to offer chances to individual colleges to show their potential for academic excellence. Neither the affiliating university gives up its responsibility for ensuring standards, nor does the State Government give up its obligations to finance higher education in autonomous colleges. The Committee stressed that autonomy has nothing to do with privatisation or commercialiation of education which are matters to be addressed by the policies of appropriate Governments.

A final issue raised in terms of reference to the Committee was about the possible problems which may arise in the implementation of the Autonomous Colleges Scheme in the State and what can be done to smoothen them in the best interests of enhanced quality of higher education in the state.

About possible problems that might arise in the implementation of autonomy, the Committee observed that for any reform which changes the established practices, there is bound to be resistance from interest groups partly because of fear of implications of anything new and partly because of ignorance of the potential for the good that the scheme involves. The resistance can be reduced if the details of the scheme are widely circulated among the stakeholders in order to remove levels of ignorance and unfounded apprehensions.

The orders issued by the Government closely followed the recommendations of the Committee and the selection of colleges was made strictly in accordance with the UGC Guidelines. The UGC sent its own teams to verify the qualifications of the selected colleges. But an ideological divide developed on the plea that autonomy would mean the Government handing over control to the colleges, particularly the aided colleges, and that the managements would play havoc with all aspects of administration. Their ability even to decide on academic matters was called into question. Although the inadequacies of the affiliation system was all too evident, sections of the teachers and students resisted the move. Even after the colleges concerned began functioning effectively, the resistance remained. The UGC teams were not allowed into the Government Colleges and the resistance continued unabated.

I was nominated by the Government to the governing councils of Mar Ivanios College and St Teresa's College, which functioned extremely well as autonomous colleges. I noticed that the universities concerned did not fully accept the status of these colleges and created hindrances to the implementation of autonomy. But some of the autonomous colleges have become model colleges and are much sought after by parents and students. Even if the new Government does not grant autonomy to more colleges, the beginning made is historic and I feel that the success of these colleges will lead to a change of heart of those who resist change.

The UGC considers autonomous colleges as harbingers of change from the outdated concept of affiliation. No university can do justice to the hundreds of colleges affiliated to them. This is the reason why there is expectation that those autonomous colleges, which function effectively will qualify for university status. Kerala has already lost precious time, and the sooner such colleges are established the better it will be for higher education in Kerala.

The universities, who were reluctant from the beginning to allow autonomy to colleges affiliated to them, have become hostile to the autonomous colleges, once they realised that the LDF Government was not in favour of autonomous colleges. The Autonomy Committee, which was formed to oversee the implementation has lapsed, leaving the colleges to wrestle with the universities through courts. The sun has set over the autonomy era even before it dawned. The autonomous colleges are in a state of crisis at the moment. The provision for autonomous colleges to be turned to universities will not apply to Kerala unless they function without hindrance for fifteen years each.

Chapter 6

STATE ASSESSMENT AND ACCREDITATION

Early in the days of the Council we envisaged a project to establish a Kerala State Assessment and Accreditation Council (KSAAC). This was done with the dual purpose of having a machinery in the state to monitor and audit the quality of higher education and also to supplement the work of the National Assessment and Accreditation Council (NAAC). This was decided on the basis of the suggestion made by the Knowledge Commission that multiple agencies may be necessary to complete the assessment and accreditation in a timely manner. Since assessment of quality is a major responsibility of the Council, a separate professional body on the lines of NAAC was considered desirable. The KSHEC Act also provides for setting up of such an agency for assessment of quality in higher education institutions.

We worked closely with NAAC in designing KSAAC. A former Chairman of NAAC, Gnanam was appointed the Chairman of a Committee formed for this purpose. The Committee consisted of five other educationists, including Jagannath Patil, Deputy Adviser, NAAC; and R Jayaprakash, a member of the Council with considerable experience of NAAC, who was the Convener of the Committee.

After extensive discussions and wide consultations with various national and international experts, the Committee made the following key recommendations, with the necessary elaboration of the vision and mission of KSAAC:

- The Kerala Government will establish the KSAAC under the provisions of KSHEC.
- Assessment and Accreditation will be voluntary to begin with, with an option to make it mandatory later in consultation with the State Government.
- Assessment and Accreditation once made will be tenable for five years. A Higher Education Institution (HEI) once accredited would be subject to the re-accreditation within one year from the date of expiration of the period of previous assessment.

The activities of KSAAC would be guided by its vision and mission that focus on making quality assurance an integral part of the functioning of higher education institutions. The vision of KSAAC was: To make quality an integral part of higher education in Kerala through a combination of self and external quality evaluation aimed at continuous quality improvement. The mission statements of the KSAAC aimed at translating KSAAC's vision into reality, defining the following key tasks of the organisation:

- To develop a Quality Assurance Framework for higher education.
- To encourage self-evaluation, accountability, autonomy and innovations in higher education including quality-related research studies.

- To involve all stakeholders of higher education for quality evaluation.
- To motivate colleges and universities for research for innovation and development of leadership qualities.
- To help institutions realise their academic objectives.

Guided by its vision and striving to achieve its mission, KSAAC would primarily aim at assessing the quality of institutions of higher education through an internationally accepted methodology, provided they were eligible to be assessed by KSAAC.

Only those educational institutes or programmes would be eligible for KSAAC assessment which would be duly approved by competent authorities and would have completed 5 years of existence.

To decide whether a unit is eligible to be assessed, KSAAC would follow a five-stage process. The five stages are:

1. Preparation and submission of a self-study report by the unit of assessment.
2. On-site visit of the peer team for validation of the self-study report and for recommending the assessment outcome to KSAAC.
3. The final decision by the Executive Committee of the KSAAC.
4. Preparation of a Continuous Quality Improvement Plan by the college/unit, based on the assessment outcome.
5. A mechanism to review the accredited institutions.

Stage 1 – Preparation of the self-study report: Institutions that fulfill the eligibility criteria would be given guidelines to prepare a self-study report to be submitted for assessment. HEIs would have their quality management systems that would continuously generate and analyse data. Self-study was thus envisaged as the backbone of the process of assessment and accreditation. There would be good harmony of internal quality system and quality assurance (QA) by KSAAC.

If a uniform methodology is evolved by the national agency all over India, the same would be adopted by KSAAC.

Stage 2 – Visit to the institution: On receiving the self-study report from the institution, KSAAC would constitute a team of peers and consult the institution about any justifiable reservation it might have about any member of the team. The peer team would visit the institution and look for patterns of evidence to validate the self-study report, through interactions with the constituents of the institution, checking documents and visiting the various units of the institution. At the end of the visit, the team would share the draft assessment report with the institution and a copy of the report, with the acceptance of the Head of the institution, would be submitted to KSAAC. The team would also give confidential scores that would decide the institutional grade.

Stage 3 – The final decision of KSAAC: The Executive Committee of KSAAC would review the report and take a decision about the grade of the institution. The grade would be valid for a period of five years.

Accreditation by KSAAC would be voluntary and for the first phase of assessment, KSAAC would take up accreditation of institutions. Subsequently, guidelines (manuals) would be developed to suit different units of higher education.

Stage 4 – Based on the assessment outcome, the college/unit would prepare Continuous Quality Improvement Plan (CQIP) to be submitted to KSAAC. This plan would have to be submitted within 6 months after the outcome of assessment.

Stage 5 – A mechanism would be developed to review and guide the accredited institutions.

The Committee identified the following core and optional criteria to serve as the basis for the assessment procedures of KSAAC.

Core Criteria

1. Curricular aspects
2. Teacher Quality
3. Teaching-Learning and Evaluation
4. Research and Consultancy
5. Infrastructure and Learning Resources
6. Student Mentoring and Support
7. Governance and Leadership

Optional Criteria

1. Community Engagement and Extension
2. Internationalisation
3. Graduate Employability Skill
4. Innovations and Good Practices

The report was approved by the Executive Council and submitted to the Government. A number of consultations were held with a view to begin the process of setting up KSAAC. In the two years that elapsed since then, NAAC decided to expand itself and continue to be the sole accreditation agency for the whole country. However, we should still have established KSAAC to audit the quality of education in Kerala. A nodal officer was appointed, but nothing substantive was done before the change of the Government.

Setting up of a monitoring and assessment agency for quality of higher education in Kerala is an absolute necessity and the report has outlined the modalities in great detail. If set up, KSAAC will evaluate the system and suggest remedies to improve the quality of education in every institution, thus enabling the Government to take appropriate action, in accordance with its needs. Even if it does not replace NAAC as an accrediting agency, we will have our own academic audit for our institutions.

Chapter 7

TEACHING THE TEACHERS

The many ills of higher education in Kerala are attributed to lack of appropriate training for the faculty before and after recruitment. Quality teachers with passion for teaching and adequate training are inevitable in any education system. The prime problem of higher education in Kerala today is dearth of quality teachers in adequate numbers. A majority of the teaching staff in higher education do not receive any formal training in teaching. Further, the rapid application and evolution of new teaching technologies present challenges to the teaching staff to stay abreast of developments while also pursuing their professional and research responsibilities. Professional development programmes are key tools that help the faculty to learn the current issues in education, better respond to cultural and systemic changes in delivery formats and refine their performance.

Hence, in-service training is necessary for the teaching staff. Such trainings are important for the following reasons:

- To help teachers keep abreast of the latest trends in higher education.

- To help teachers recognise the different capabilities of students and modify the method of teaching accordingly.
- To recognise and master the use of modern teaching aids so as to make the teaching and learning processes more lively and useful.

Teachers in the primary and secondary education sectors have structured pre-service and in-service training obligations and interventions, but this is lacking in the field of higher education. In higher education, the teachers are selected on the basis of proficiency in the subject and are not trained in teaching skills before getting inducted into teaching.

The Council decided to address this issue by setting up a Committee with Babu Joseph, former Vice Chancellor of Cochin University of Science and Technology (CUSAT), as its Chairman. The Committee proposed the setting up of a Faculty Training Academy to fulfill the need for imparting professional training to all teachers of higher education at the induction level itself. Follow-up programmes for senior teachers at wellspaced intervals was also to be taken up by the Academy. The objectives of the Academy included:

1. To ensure quality improvement in higher education by setting high standards for teaching by enhancing teachers' competencies in terms of academic excellence, research orientation and teaching skill through rigorous training.
2. To impart professional training at the induction level so as to generate professionalism which would be helpful to the individuals throughout the service.
3. To equip the teachers with necessary competencies, skills and attitudes which would enable them to face the international challenges effectively.

The Committee proposed that the Academy should have the status of a university with the capacity to train 2000 teachers at different stages per year. It should be fully residential and located in Thiruvananthapuram in a campus of 50 acres. As for the administrative structure, it was proposed that the Academy should function under the direct supervision of the KSHEC with a nominated Governing Body, consisting of experts and Officials.

The training would be imparted to both newly recruited and senior teachers. The newly recruited teachers would undergo induction training for three months and the senior teachers would be trained in different modules of varying duration.

The Committee recommended that:

- The curriculum should include effective communication skills, pedagogy, use of teaching aids and techniques, value education, mentoring, leadership, ICT applications, statistical analysis, research orientation and instrument handling, preparation of project proposals and evaluation, concept papers, question paper setting and evaluation of curriculum development, environmental awareness, organising seminars, conferences and workshops, etc.
- The teachers should be trained for hard work, commitment, positive attitude, analytical skills, communication skills, entrepreneurial skills, motivation, inspiration, facilitation, competitiveness, honesty integrity, dedication, punctuality, discipline, human rights, gender sensitisation and commitment to social justice.

The induction training shall be mandatory for the faculty of all teachers in university departments, affiliated/recognised colleges at the Assistant Professor or equivalent level and the duration of training shall be part of their probation period.

The probation period of the candidates shall not be declared unless they successfully complete the training.

Even before the report of the Committee became available, the then Chief Minister Oommen Chandy had taken up the proposal with the then Human Resource Development (HRD) Minister at a meeting in Kasaragod. The Minister fully endorsed the idea and agreed to provide the funding. The report was immediately approved by the Government, but it ran into rough weather because of the intense lobbying by some people for heading the Academy. At one point, I had to go to the Education Minister to stop an unsuitable person being appointed and, as a result, machinations started to take the Academy out of the administrative control of the KSHEC. An order was actually issued to this effect, stating that the KSHEC would be too preoccupied with other matters to take care of the Academy. Here I put my foot down and got the order annulled. As a consequence, the Department of Higher Education turned hostile to the project and virtually killed it by diversionary tactics. Even after the Sanskrit University offered space to start the Academy, the idea was shelved under some pretext or another.

It is a sad commentary on the state of affairs that even a matter of urgency like training of faculty was sabotaged by vested interests with the connivance of the bureaucracy. This is a project that should be revived as soon as possible in the interest of higher education in the state.

Pending the establishment of a professional institution for training of faculty of our universities and colleges, I have been suggesting a simple way to train the young recruits to the teaching profession. In the initial days, the recruits should be invited to sit in the classes of senior teachers to observe their classes and to discuss the techniques that each one uses after each class. But I was told that neither the seniors nor the juniors are enthusiastic about such a method. This again appears to be a mindset issue, which needs to be resolved.

Chapter 8

INDUSTRY AND ACADEMIA AS PARTNERS

Having seen the close beneficial collaboration between the academic institutions and the industrial houses in planning, funding courses and building academic infrastructure in other countries. I was anxious to explore possibilities for similar linkages in Kerala. In the present system, the industry plays virtually no role in planning or funding education. The industry goes to higher education institutions for campus recruitment and takes away the best graduates as a favour to the institutions. Very often, they also complain that the graduates are unemployable without further professional training. Ideally, the industrial houses should determine the kind of graduates they require and also fund the courses designed by them for specific jobs. Moreover, the industry could assist in providing internships to students and also send corporate leaders to interact with them. Opportunities for the faculty to familiarise themselves with corporate decision-making could also help.

The higher education system in Kerala has lost its comparative advantage in education eroding over time, and the majority of its students are ill-equipped to deal with globalised market demand. There is also an endemic concern expressed by industry that the output of the higher education system is ill-trained and needs considerable remedial training before they can be productive. Given relatively low levels of industrialisation, Kerala has been troubled by educated unemployment in the past; if there is a slowdown in overseas migration, we may again see unemployment and under-employment rising in the State.

It is in this context that a Committee on Industry–Academia Linkages was constituted with Rajeev Srinivasan as its Chairman and other prominent academics and industry experts as its members.

As per the terms of reference, the Committee considered various approaches towards creating mechanisms to induce students, industry and academia to engage meaningfully with each other.

After holding six meetings, the Committee arrived at a series of recommendations in several broad categories. They also held one interaction with the IT industry. The general thrust of the recommendations was on the following:

1. Creating conditions that improve the interactions between industry, academia, research labs and students as well as skill upgrading.
2. Creating mechanisms that will increase the level of structured innovation and entrepreneurship so that more students from Kerala become job-creators rather than job-seekers, especially in sectors where the State has a comparative advantage.
3. Using the fast-moving technology of education in ways that can make it feasible to update students with the latest course.

The report of the Committee was submitted to the Government and circulated to the universities and industries, pointing out that most recommendations could be implemented without any action by the Government. Some engineering colleges and business schools warmly welcomed the report and acted in accordance with its recommendations.

One obvious disadvantage in Kerala is that it has very few manufacturing industries and the IT companies have a set pattern in which they operate. But the recommendations of the Committee, in which the Ministry of Human Resource Development (MHRD) was represented, should serve as a guide to establish Academia-Industry linkages for the benefit of higher education.

Chapter 9

FEAR OF PRIVATISATION

In its quest for excellence in higher education, Kerala has confronted a number of problems such as dearth of financial resources, lack of modern and dynamic institutions and shortage of gifted faculty. Unfortunately, an avenue to solve these problems, identified by the UGC and adopted by other States in India, the establishment of private universities, had not been explored by the Government of Kerala so far. The Council felt that the time had come to study the feasibility of establishing private universities in Kerala, particularly in the light of offers from some institutions inside and outside Kerala to set up such universities.

The need for private universities was emphasised by many delegates from India and abroad at an International Meet on Transnational Education (TNE) organised by the Council in January 2014. They said private universities with an innovative spirit, without the constraints of state universities, might be able to work freely with foreign universities and derive the benefits of collaboration with world-class universities. Accordingly, the Thiruvananthapuram Declaration, which contained the recommendations of the Meet, proposed a feasibility study on the establishment of private universities. When this was reported in the press at that time, the Education Minister stated in the Assembly that the Government had no plans to set up private universities.

Subsequently, the Minister visited Dubai Academic City and was dazzled by it. Without realising that most of the universities there were private, he proposed a similar Academic City and dispatched a three-member team to study the possibilities. The team also proposed such an Academic City consisting of institutions with linkages with foreign universities in the self-financing mode, without realising that such institutions would not contemplate affiliation with the existing state universities. No action was taken on the report for a long time.

The Chief Minister called late in the evening one day and told me that the Archbishop of Thrissur was on his way to my home on his suggestion to discuss the setting up of a private university in Kerala. I agreed to meet him, but told the Chief Minister that legislation would be necessary to set up private universities. I also said that the first step would be to study the feasibility of setting up private universities. After I met the Archbishop, I suggested a study, particularly since we had a specific proposal before us. Knowing the views of the Education Minister, I spoke to him about the study. He was not enthusiastic, but said that there was no harm in doing a study.

The Council secured the services of some eminent academicians and others under the leadership of Cyriac Thomas to undertake a study of the feasibility of establishing private universities in Kerala. The report submitted by the Committee, after extensive consultations and intensive discussions, covers all aspects of the issue, including the likely roadblocks and difficulties, which are special to Kerala. The Committee was unanimous in its opinion that setting up of private universities in Kerala is extremely desirable and eminently possible. It has noted that even those who expressed reservations are not fundamentally opposed to the idea. They have merely voiced their apprehension that, in the current social and political climate in Kerala, private universities may face several problems, which are enumerated in the report.

Private universities have been envisaged as new generation institutions, which will have innovative methods of teaching, the most modern frontiers of knowledge, without being bogged down by the outdated procedures and other constraints associated with some of the older universities. Sufficient safeguards have been built in to enable the State to regulate the functioning of these universities so that they become an integral part of the plans and purposes of the State.

The Committee identified the advantages of private universities in the following terms:

> Private universities can attempt to create a higher education system that ranks among the world's leading education systems and which will enable Kerala to compete in the global economy. Such universities:
>
> - Will bring in considerable private funds for the advancement of higher education, reducing the Government's burden.
> - Will have to rely on excellence and quality to ensure survival and therefore will be continually responsive to emerging trends.
> - Can instil an entrepreneurial mindset in higher education system and create a system that produces qualified personnel with a drive to create jobs, rather than mere job seekers searching for a livelihood.
> - Will construct a system that is less focused on traditional,

academic pathways and places an equal value on the much-needed technological skills, career and professional training.

- Can focus on outcomes over inputs and actively pursue technologies and innovations that address students' needs and enable greater personalisation of the learning experience.
- Will enable transition from the current, highly centralised governance system to a new model based on academic autonomy within the regulatory framework which prevents wanton abuse.
- Will ensure the financial sustainability of the higher education system by asking all stakeholders that directly benefit from it to contribute their share.
- Can enhance the students' learning experience by expanding industry collaboration in the design and delivery of programmes, increasing the use of experiential and service learning to develop modern skills, and leveraging technology-enabled models to enable more personalised learning.
- Will enable the industry to lead curriculum design and delivery through new partnership models and raising the quality of delivery through increased apprenticeship, hands-on training, real-life simulations, and specialised employer training programmes.
- Will focus on creating scale and growth in a few strategic research areas which are linked to national priorities for economic growth.
- Will promote the flow of students from abroad, particularly from West Asia, South Asia and East Africa, by diversifying and raising the quality of niche programmes.

Apart from establishing the structure, the nature of the innovative courses and research projects, the Committee dwelt at length on the various positions in the private universities and the method of selecting personnel for those positions, taking care to provide the safeguards against any unfair practices even by the investors themselves. Regulations were suggested, taking into account the following risk factors:

- The private universities, being new in Kerala, will face many problems in their establishment and operations. All the existing universities in Kerala are owned and operated by the State. It will take time for the public to accept the concept of a private university. Also many private players, including some with no credentials in the education sector, may come forward to establish a private university. This will give rise to demands for rigorous regulation.
- The university has to attract students. In the initial years, the parents may have apprehensions about the validity and acceptance of the academic certification issued by a private university. This may discourage enrollments initially.
- A private university, by definition, has to be self-supportive. This will necessitate levying higher fees to cover the actual expenses. Having been used to a low-fee structure in governmental and aided institutions, many may not prefer to do courses in a private university because of higher fees. Therefore, many meritorious students may go elsewhere where fees are less.
- Being operated by private agencies, the universities will not survive for long unless they are financially sound and viable, or unless the sponsoring agency is able to pump in a lot of resources for a long time. Consequently, there is a danger of the institution collapsing. Such an eventuality will create serious difficulties for students and faculty.
- At the other extreme, such a university can also be used as a profit centre for extracting maximum amount of money through fees. This might lead to widespread profiteering.

Therefore, it is mandatory and necessary that the system of private university is well regulated to effectively guard against the risks. The Draft Bill suggested for adoption by the legislature to take care of all these eventualities and outlined the measures, which have to be put in place.

The spread of modern education elsewhere and lack of high quality higher and professional educational opportunities and employment opportunities in Kerala have forced many people, especially the talented and skilled youth who aspire for quality higher education, to migrate in search of academic avenues to neighbouring States and also to universities abroad, especially to Singapore, Malaysia, USA, UK, Europe, Canada, Australia, etc.

Inclusion and excellence in higher education are the major thrust areas in the 12th Five-Year Plan. It is also necessary to increase the gross enrolment ratio of students in order to accelerate the development prospects of India. But this might remain only a dream if the nation continues to depend only on state-run educational institutions. The State is seriously handicapped in the matter of the huge financial resources which will be required to be invested for improving the quality of higher education. So, private agencies have a definitive role to play in this regard.

The well-established educational agencies in Kerala having strengths, capacities and capabilities, such as experienced management, involvement of committed professionals, a successful track record, experience in technical and professional education, a strong brand name, and teams of qualified and dedicated human resources who are willing to support them, may be encouraged to develop private universities in the State. Such institutions should aspire, and also be encouraged, to be landmark institutions in the country, competing and ranking with the best in the world.

The proposal for permitting private universities in Kerala got highly politicised even when the Committee was studying the issue. An International Conference on Transnational Education organised by the Council in 2014 had made a recommendation in its Thiruvananthapuram Declaration that establishment of private universities should be studied as part of quality enhancement efforts. But the Minister of Education stated in the Assembly that there was no proposal in the Government for private universities. However, the Government announced in the Budget speech for 2015-16 that International Higher Education Zones would be established, with considerable private participation to house educational institutions with international linkages. It was obvious that such institutions could not be affiliated to state universities. I suggested, therefore, that we should study the proposal for private universities in this context. The Chief Minister approved the study. The Education Minister, however, maintained his opposition, though he did not want to stand in the way of a study. Throughout the course of the study, he publicly stated that he was not in favour of private universities.

When the report was finalised, the Chief Minister suggested that I should hand over the report to him in the presence of the Education Minister. Accordingly, a meeting was arranged and the Chief Minister suggested that the report should be discussed by the Cabinet and an all-party conference before taking a view on it. The Education Minister agreed, but after the photo opportunity of my presenting the report, he told the press that he was opposed to private universities! The Chief Minister was confident that the proposal would eventually go through, but the whole thing was shelved for lack of time as the elections drew closer. The objection of the Education Minister was difficult to understand as he or his party, the Muslim League, had no ideological opposition to private investment in education. Apparently, he was bargaining for support for the establishment of an Arabic University as a quid pro quo. But the opponents of private universities benefitted from the impasse in the Government and an opportunity to establish private universities was lost in the process.

I have no doubt that private universities will come into being in Kerala sooner than later. That is the only way we can have a new generation of universities with quality education. The State will not have the kind of resources required to build such universities. I hope that the work done by the Council on this issue will be found useful at that time.

Chapter 10

A UNIVERSITY FOR THE POLICE

The idea of a Police University in addition to, and distinct from, the Police Training Academy was the brainchild of the Home Minister, Ramesh Chennithala. Even before taking up the matter with the Government, the Home Minister visited NR Madhava Menon at his home and requested him to prepare the groundwork for establishing a Police University. It was Menon who suggested that the KSHEC should be entrusted with the responsibility of giving him support and guidance. Accordingly, the Department of Higher Education requested me to form a Committee and study the issue and submit a report. Only a very broad outline of the objectives was given to us.

The KSHEC set up the Committee, as desired by the Government, on 18 March 2014. The Committee met six times and also held consultations with the concerned Ministers and Experts at the local and national levels. The report, mostly written by Menon, reflects the consensus in the Committee on all aspects of the proposal. Former DGP, Jacob Punnoose, contributed the chapter on the need for a Police University.

The university being proposed in the report is unique in many ways and it 'has the potential to become a world-class institution of its kind,' as stated by the Chairman in his forwarding letter addressed to me. The report recommended the setting up of the National University for Police Sciences and Security Studies (NUPSAS). The report consists of a Draft Bill, Explanatory Notes by the Chairman, a Project Report and a Draft Budget.

The report makes it clear that while police and policing will be central to its functioning, the university is conceived to be more broad-based to comprehend security in all its dimensions, some of which may, for example, fall in such varied domains as communications, aviation, health, environment, and trade and commerce. Internal security, it pointed out, goes far beyond police and policing in the conventional sense and should include issues such as the Maoist/Naxalite movement, challenges of fundamentalism and communal forces, insurgency in border areas, drug addiction and trafficking, terrorist incursions from across the border, illegal infiltrations and settlement of foreigners, civil disobedience, organised crime with global ramifications, regional separatism movements, etc. These issues warrant strategic thinking and action involving knowledge and skills across disciplines and domains, which a university of the kind proposed should be able to address upfront.

The university will be a national non-affiliating university, admitting students to different courses of study at the undergraduate and postgraduate levels, and involved in cutting-edge research on security-related issues. The university is intended not only for teaching, research and training but also to assist the Central and State Governments in policy planning, policy evaluation, programme development and problem-solving in security-related issues. It will act as a 'think tank' for professional management of internal security and constitutional governance under the rule of law.

The university is to be a truly autonomous body maintaining world-class standards with guidance from an Advisory Council comprising of security experts chosen from across the world.

Unlike other universities in the State, NUPSAS is statutorily obliged to raise at least 50 per cent of its budgetary requirements through its own efforts. This is expected to give it some amount of financial autonomy as well.

Though the Police University must not become a Police Academy with a new name, it must also significantly contribute towards improving the Academy's training inputs relating to policing and security sciences, and also serve to improve the knowledge level of those who become police professionals. The university will have a dual role—first, that of a distinct academic entity structured as a centre of higher learning, quite separate from that of the Police Academy; and secondly, that of a significant change agent in enhancing the quality of policing by improving the intellectual capacity and academic knowledge-level of the police personnel. The university must ultimately stand for the betterment of policing, but it must not primarily be of the police and by the police. In short, the university must be an academic institution, run by competent academicians in a healthy academic environment for the betterment of policing and security sciences.

The administrative structure and official hierarchy established for the university will be in line with the IITs and IIMs rather than the State university, with specific roles for the Governor, Chief Minister and the Home Minister.

The report was presented to the Chief Minister, but the senior bureaucracy promptly pointed out that the Police Academy was sufficient, without even examining the kind of responsibilities entrusted to the university. However, subsequently, a Special Officer was appointed by the UDF Government and another by the LDF Government to start the preparatory work. In spite of that, the university is nowhere near conceptualisation, not to speak of implementation.

Chapter 11

RUSA IN RUINS

> Rashtriya Uchchatar Shiksha Abhiyan (RUSA) is a Centrally Sponsored Scheme (CSS), launched in 2013, aimed at providing strategic funding to eligible state higher educational institutions. The central funding (in the ratio of 60:40 for general category States, 90:10 for special category States and 100% for Union Territories) would be norm-based and outcome-dependent. The funding would flow from the Central Ministry through the State Governments/Union Territories to the State Higher Education Councils before reaching the identified institutions. The funding to States would be made on the basis of critical appraisal of the state higher education plans, which would describe each state's strategy to address the issues of equity, access and excellence in higher education.
>
> —MHRD

RUSA was meant to transform the state higher education institutions, with sufficient funding. It was repeatedly stated in the RUSA document that the responsibility for formulating an overall State plan, receiving the proposals from the institutions, seeking of funds, allocation of funds and monitoring of the implementation will be the responsibility of the State Higher Education Councils. Guidelines were also given to reconstitute the Councils in due course to meet the additional requirements.

RUSA would create new universities through upgradation of the existing autonomous colleges and conversion of colleges in a cluster. It would create new model degree colleges, new professional colleges and provide infrastructural support to universities and colleges. Faculty recruitment support, faculty improvement programmes and leadership development of educational administrators are also an important part of the scheme. In order to enhance skill development, the existing central scheme of polytechnics has been subsumed within RUSA. A separate component to synergize vocational education with higher education has also been included in RUSA. Besides these, RUSA also supports reforming, restructuring and building the capacity of institutions in participating States.

The Department of Higher Education saw in the creation of RUSA a threat to its absolute authority in fund allocation and began a turf battle with the KSHEC right from the beginning. Everything relating to RUSA was delayed even though the time was running out for formulating the plans and for seeking funds. After about a year, at the intervention of the Chief Minister, an order was issued, designating the Council as the implementing agency for RUSA, but nothing was done, except to ask the Council to formulate a plan. The Department continued to correspond with the MHRD and passed on some instructions from time to time. We held workshops, received institutional plans, prepared a plan with the help of a Technical Support Group set up by us. As a result of the delaying tactics of the Department, the preparatory work was done within the budget of the Council, saving up the preparatory fund. However, this resulted in criticism by the MHRD that the preparatory funds were not spent; they also indicated that the States that did not spend the preparatory grant would not be given the full infrastructure grant. My proposal to debit the preparatory work done by us to the RUSA funds fell on deaf ears. By the time the Department agreed to debit the expenses on some of the studies done by the Council, the time had passed for us to gain any advantage.

The Council submitted a detailed set of proposals, encompassing the projects we had prepared, such as the Accreditation Council, the Faculty Training Academy, the Police Science University and a Research and Innovation University. But the MHRD kept shifting the goal posts and made these proposals ineligible for funding. All new projects were excluded from consideration and new universities could not be proposed. Eventually, a meagre allocation was made only for infrastructure. The amount was allocated to 5 universities and 15 Government colleges on the basis of their proposals, including renovation. But the schedule for implementation was so tight that no worthwhile progress was made in the given time. Thus, further grants were ruled out for the time being.

The Department and the MHRD began to conspire to exclude the Council from RUSA implementation. They did not take action to reconstitute the Council, on the basis of RUSA recommendations, which I had proposed right from the beginning. Instead, they began to spread rumours that RUSA could not be implemented as long as an academic was not at its head, though MHRD had given two years' time to reconstitute the Council. In any event, there was a provision that someone with extensive experience in any profession could head the Council. Still, reports appeared that RUSA was stuck because of the composition of the Council, and even a question regarding this was asked in the assembly, which the Minister did not refute.

What followed was an unethical move by the Department to sabotage the role of the Council with the connivance of the Member Secretary and two others in the Council. They were plotting to get themselves transferred to the RUSA unit in the hope of getting longer terms and larger salaries and their grievance was that I had not agreed to transfer them to the RUSA unit. Suddenly, a State Coordinator for RUSA was appointed and he began to undermine the Council by cultivating the Member Secretary and a Research Officer and an IT Specialist. They hatched a plot to get themselves relieved from the Council. The Member Secretary, on a day when I was out of town, sent a 'no objection certificate' for the relieving of the persons concerned, as requested by the Department, and did not inform me about it. Having tied up their transfer, they told me that they wanted to revert to their parent institutions to which I readily agreed, because I could see that they were up to mischief. When I was told that they were being appointed to the RUSA unit, I protested to the Minister and refused to relieve them. The Minister agreed, but soon issued an order that they should be relieved. The whole episode was conspiratorial and against civilised behaviour and bureaucratic norms. The fact that the conspirators included the high officials in the Department of Higher Education shocked me beyond words. But I did not make an issue of it because I did not want to add to the turf battles and bad blood in the bureaucracy. It taught me a lesson not to trust even my own officers. This was in sharp contrast to my experience with the External Affairs bureaucracy, which was generally loyal and conscientious.

RUSA was virtually in ruins as a result of these machinations and no additional allocation was made to Kerala till I left the Council in April 2016. The expectation that sufficient funding would be available to bring in reforms was not fulfilled. Much of the responsibility for this sad State of affairs rested squarely on the Department of Higher Education. The strategy was one of subterfuge and not direct confrontation. All concerned pretended to be polite and friendly, but stooped to the lowest levels of behaviour to attain their ends. The RUSA episode was typical of the situation in Kerala, which is a curse of the State. This also explains the constant bickering even among the senior bureaucrats, leading to the rise of the conspirators and the fall of the conscientious ones.

The surprising point about the RUSA episode was that the lower bureaucracy was able to overturn decisions taken at the Cabinet level in Delhi. For the unscrupulous officers, nothing is sacrosanct and they manipulate decision-making by using the 'Yes Minister' technique. Very often, the personal staff of the Ministers are willing collaborators. Kerala has no hope of realising its full potential unless the bureaucratic evils are controlled, if not eradicated. The RUSA episode is an eloquent expression of what ails our system.

Chapter 12

SAMAAGATI: GENDER JUSTICE ON CAMPUS

A major initiative of the KSHEC was a study of gender justice in campuses in Kerala called the *Samaagati* Report by a Committee headed by a national expert, Meenakshi Gopinath. The Committee consisted of experts and activists from the fields of academia, law, media, psychology, and NGOs in Kerala. The purpose of the Committee was to highlight the factors contributing to the present 'unsatisfactory situation and recommend a set of measures to be put in place' as remedies.

The adoption of the *Saksham* Report on 'Measures for Ensuring the Safety of Women' and 'Programmes for Gender Sensitisation on Campuses,' by the UGC in early 2014, along with its far-reaching recommendations for HEIs to implement measures for gender equality and equity in universities and colleges, has received wide attention. The recommendations are based broadly on the principles of equality and justice guaranteed by the Constitution, including the Right to Dignity, Bodily Autonomy and Integrity enunciated in the Bill of Rights for Women in the Justice Verma Committee Report of January 2013 and other relevant Acts.

The Report has recommended measures to give effect to the policy of zero tolerance of gender-based violence on all campuses. Through highly innovative programmes, including a special course on gender sensitisation and a series of shorter workshops on gender, masculinities, combating sexual harassment and imparting legal rights, the Report offers modules that can be disseminated widely to all HEIs. Conducting Open Forums on an ongoing basis is another innovative mechanism recommended to achieve accountability and enlist the involvement of all members of higher education institutions in the task of imparting equality, dignity and the ability to live, work and study without the fear of harassment and violence.

The KSHEC had participated in the deliberative process of the SAKSHAM Report and also in its fact-finding proceedings through an Open Forum of Stakeholders in HEIs in the April of 2013. It also participated in a workshop of coordinators and students of Women Empowerment Cells in universities and colleges in February 2015. The inputs received were an eye-opener and revealed that campuses in Kerala are far from free in matters of gender discrimination, exploitation, harassment and deep-seated prejudices against women. Despite communications from the UGC, the MHRD and the State Government to put in place effective measures and mechanisms to combat these, the ground situation in the universities and colleges leaves a great deal to be desired.

Kerala that boasts to be among the States with the highest literacy rates in the country and Positive Human Development Indicators suggesting progressive advances in the social sector, sadly, reflects a stark lack of sensitivity to gender issues on its campuses and institutions of higher education. Of particular concern is the prevalence of the culture of silence and of impunity on issues of gender-based violence and an alarming acceptance of misogyny legitimised in institutional and administrative arrangements within the higher education space. For Kerala society, this contradiction indicates a regressive trend.

KSHEC organised a workshop in Kerala where, both at the operational and the ideational level, the participants highlighted several prevalent issues, and exhorted that immediate remedial measures be put in place to stem the alarming tide of gender-based discrimination, bias and prejudice in the policies and practices of educational institutions. Among the startling factors that came to the notice of the Committee were attitudes and practices, various kinds of harassment, unavailability of grievance-handling mechanisms, lack of support systems, lack of infra-structure amenities and paucity of robust academic programmes for gender sensitisation.

The Committee made a set of recommendations, in keeping with the relevant laws and in the light of the specific issues raised by the stakeholders, giving a role to the KSHEC to transmit the findings to the HEIs and to help implement them. The Report was presented to the Governing Council of KSHEC, which has as its members all Vice Chancellors of the universities, but they were in a denial mode, despite the specificity of the charges and the judgment of the Committee itself. They agreed to look into the allegations, but claimed that the whole issue was grossly exaggerated.

The *Samaagati* Report, a clear indictment of the universities about the treatment of women on the campuses and an agenda for action, remains unimplemented, even as more and more instances of harassment come to light. The KSHEC should take up the implementation of the Report to tackle the urgent issues facing the campuses.

Chapter 13

ARABIC AS AN ASSET

A proposal to study the specific problems of Arabic colleges came to me from the Education Minister. A Committee was constituted, with the Member Secretary of the KSHEC as its Chairman. While briefing the Committee, I suggested to them that they should not only examine the present problems of Arabic education but also think in terms of establishing an International Arabic University. I was not aware about the earlier proposals in this regard and suggested it as a logical thing to do, following the interaction of Kerala with the Gulf countries. I felt that the present employer–employee relationship should be transformed into a political, economic and cultural relationship, and the Arabic language, in which there is already considerable proficiency in Kerala, could serve as one of the instruments for this. I did not see it as a regional or religious issue. The Committee followed up my proposal and submitted a Report, in which they built a case for an Arabic University.

Over the past few decades, the importance of Arabic as a global language has received an added fillip thanks to the emergence of the Middle East as an important commercial and cultural hub of the world. As an important economic and cultural centre, the Middle East occupies a prominent place in the modern world.

The ties between India and the Arab world predate our emergence as nation States. Proofs of the presence of the Arabs in India can be traced out from the pre-Islamic ages. It is proved in the full light of history that Arabia, even though it was a part of the East, acted as a link between the Indian subcontinent and the rest of the world and enjoyed a monopoly in the world trade for centuries. Commodities produced or found in India were introduced to the world by the Arab merchants.

Settlement of Arabs in the southwestern coastal areas of India continued even after the spread of Islam. These increased settlements have paved the way for the formation of a new social group in Malabar called 'Mappilas.' There were a number of cultural contributions for the Arab settlers and Mappilas in the linguistic, literary, cultural and social spheres of Kerala throughout history. For instance, before the reforms made by Ezhuthachan in the Malayalam script, Arabic script was used to write Malayalam and Tamil. It is interesting to note the fact that the first book on the history of Kerala, by a Keralite (Sheikh Zainuddin Makhdoom) was written in pure Arabic. Following this, a number of scholars from Kerala wrote books in Arabic, in an array of religious as well as secular subjects.

There are studies that reveal the literary and cultural contributions of Indians, who settled permanently or virtually in Arabia over the past several centuries. At present, there are millions of Indians working in the Gulf-Arab countries and most of them are from Kerala.

The proposed Arabic university would be a giant step in reclaiming the spirit of fraternity between this southwestern coastal area of India and the Arab world. Keralites working in the Gulf countries constitute the bulwark of Kerala economy. According to available data, the total contribution of Non-Resident Keralites based in the Gulf countries to the state economy was a whopping Rs 75,000 crore in the year 2013. Kerala households directly depend on income from the Gulf countries for their livelihood. The number of indirect beneficiaries would work out to nearly 80 per cent of the population of Kerala.

Keralites enjoy a major part of the advantage in the overseas job markets owing to their knowledge of Arabic, a language that seeped into the cultural geography of Kerala through contacts ante-dating the advent of Islam in India. It is an interesting fact to note that the Arabic script was widely used in Kerala to write Malayalam until the spelling reforms in the 15th century.

The proposed Arabic University can be considered as an appropriate response to a historical and cultural need of the present trajectory. Besides training Arabic students and prospective job seekers, it will also play a vital role in re-assembling, researching and marshalling the invaluable knowledge concerning Kerala and Indian history recorded in Arabic manuscripts by travellers and scholars.

The university will thus be able to contribute positively to the growth of knowledge and learning, apart from chopping new pathways in fostering greater intra and inter-cultural dialogue.

The KSHEC found the report eminently reasonable and we submitted it to the Government. A wide debate started immediately thereafter, and the arguments and counter-arguments made earlier came back to life. I was invited by many groups and institutions to discuss the issue and I maintained my support, making it clear that I was seeing it purely in the context of India's relations with the Arab world. But it was argued that an Arabic University would be a nest of terrorists. I pointed out how Islamic Centres functioned in world cities like Washington and that it would be wrong to identify terrorism with a language or religion.

I came to know from press reports that senior officials in the Kerala Government strongly objected to the Arabic University and the matter was set aside, in spite of strong pressure from certain quarters. I hope that, like other path-breaking proposals, Kerala will come round to accept the setting up of an Arabic University, once it transcends its false fears and gets ready to achieve larger goals.

Chapter 14

A POLICY FOR HIGHER EDUCATION

The KSHEC felt that there was a need to review the State Higher Education Policy prepared by the previous Council to make higher education more liberal and purposeful. A Committee was established under the chairmanship of JAK Tareen to go into all aspects of the current status of the higher education system in the State and to make holistic recommendations for reforms not only to bring in correctional measures in the existing academic, administrative and infrastructural shortcomings, but also recommend such fundamental structural changes that would enhance the quality of teaching and research not only to meet the needs of the state and the nation, but to become globally competitive.

The Committee carefully went through the various policy documents on education, brought out from time to time, including the most recent Knowledge Commission Report and Professor Yash Pal Committee Report on Higher Education and the Report submitted by Professor UR Ananthmurthy Committee to the Council. Some of the issues brought out by the earlier reports pertain to dilution of the basic philosophy of university education caused due to fragmentation of education, commercialisation of education and lack of appropriate regulatory mechanisms. All the previous Reports had expressed concern about the falling standards both in teaching and research in universities and colleges. Enhancing research and teaching standards, improving the quality of teachers and attracting good teachers is yet another challenge before the country.

The Committee recognised the positive dividends as well as the pitfalls brought into the system with the explosive growth of the private institutions in the recent past. The Committee also recognised the need for more focused and action-oriented recommendations that would give clarity to the Government on the required actions to be initiated in a phased manner. Hence, the report took into account the spirit of all the earlier reports but recommended a practical action plan to bring about the desired changes in higher education in the State of Kerala.

The Committee viewed with great concern that Kerala is not a preferred destination for students from other States and international community, while most of the other States attract students from across the country. A number of reforms and structural changes were suggested by the Committee not only to flush the state with a fresh breeze of innovation in higher education, but also to make Kerala a sought-after destination by the students from across the nation and international community.

The Report was in the form of a number of options to choose from, depending on political will, academic acceptability and availability of funds. The Council chose the following recommendations of the Committee for immediate implementation.

The vision for the State during the next 25 years shall be:

- to increase access to higher education and research;
- to enhance the quality of education and research;
- to ensure equity in higher education.

In order to achieve these objectives, the Council made the following recommendations:

To Increase Access

- Infrastructure expansion and increase in the intake capacities of colleges and universities by 50 per cent in the next five years and by 100 per cent in next 10 years, in subjects/programmes of relevance and high demand.
- Establishing new colleges in Malapuram, Palakkad, Wayanad, Kasargod and Idukki districts, as there is no access to college education in the vicinity.
- Establishing at least one women's university in the State and 10 women's colleges.
- Establishing a State University for Distance Education (Open University) based on public-private partnership (PPP) where sharing of revenue should be approved by the Distance Education Council, Delhi, and the degrees to be awarded should be distinguished from those of the regular day programmes.
- Exploring possibilities by institutions to introduce evening programmes both at the college and the university level, wherever feasible.
- Encouraging colleges with substantial standing and reputation to apply for autonomous status to be given by the UGC.

- Every college to have at least one hostel for boys and one for girl students.

To Enhance the Quality of Higher Education

- Adhering to the teacher-student ratio approved by the UGC. This requires optimum teacher ratio for all disciplines. In postgraduate programmes, for sciences 1:10-12; for arts, humanities, social sciences and commerce 1:15. For undergraduate programmes, in sciences 1:30 and in others 1:40.
- Offering courses on environment and ecology; philosophy, ethics and morals; human rights and Indian political system; and history of Indian culture and traditional knowledge at all degree programmes including professional colleges.
- Constituting a Committee to prescribe the minimum standards and lay down the norms to be followed for maintaining quality of laboratory and infrastructure.
- Establishing Kerala State Library Network (KSLNET) to treat library modernisation, library staff training, networking of libraries, digitalisation as a priority area for improvement of teaching and research programmes.
- Introducing a massive e-learning educational portal.
- Bidding by the State of Kerala for the establishment of a regional sophisticated instrumentation centre funded by UGC in select zones during the 12th Plan with part contribution from the Government and part from the UGC.
- Establishing a Sports Development Academy and a State Sports Training Centre in the State.

- Integrating the undergraduate programmes with the postgraduate programmes; upgrading the standalone colleges to PG colleges in a phased manner.
- Establishing separate universities for Law and Indian traditional medicine.
- Abolishing the affiliation system and establishing 'college cluster multi-campus universities' (CCMCU).
- Introducing a State accreditation system (KSAAC) for accreditation and ranking.

To Ensure Equity in Higher Education

- Introducing a stricter monitoring mechanism and to bring in transparency into the system to prevent possible manipulations and conversions of seats and opportunities meant for the SC/ST/OBC/minorities and other beneficiaries.
- Establishing a State Higher Educational Tribunal empowered to remedy any complaints relating to discrimination or denial of opportunity.
- Enhancing the autonomy of universities and reducing State control into the day-to-day working of the universities and colleges, if necessary, by way of an amendment to the present Act.
- Nomination of the Government representatives to the academic bodies and representation of the Government on the senate and executive council/syndicate should be through nomination of persons who are experts in the field of educational/research institutions, public sector, judiciary, industry, or such persons whose presence would contribute to the governance of the university.

- Inclusion of representatives of the teaching community on the academic and all other bodies of the private management, in addition to the members from the management.
- Evolving a mechanism to constrain political interference in academic institution in matters of academics and administration and to uphold complete academic and financial autonomy of the universities and the Vice Chancellors.
- Introducing a common academic calendar stating the date of re-opening for an academic year, dates of examinations to be completed, timeline for the announcement of results and uniform date for closing of admissions in the State.
- Introducing a Universities Act in the State upholding the autonomy of universities and Vice Chancellors, enhancing the overall powers of the Syndicate and a having common academic council to monitor and set standards for the academic affairs of the universities in Kerala.
- Preventing unfair practices and nepotism in all appointments of teachers to aided, and Government colleges and ensuring a high standard in the selection of teachers. Framing of guidelines for the selection of the faculty by self-financing institutions in order to ensure heterogeneity and fair representation.
- A suggested amendment to KSHEC Act, 2007, will be submitted, so that the State Council shall be entrusted with the additional responsibility and powers in all matters relating to the quality of higher education, preventing unfair practices and regulating the need of minimum infrastructure, etc.

- The state should explore the possibility of establishing specialised research centres such as the Centre for Policy and Developmental Studies and Statistical Analysis which would be a single window source for the Government in formulating all its policy plans, assessment of performance, comprehensive statistical data and analysis of every institution and Schemes of the Government.

Chapter 15

UNIFORM ACT FOR UNIVERSITIES

The establishment of various universities over a period of several years resulted in different Acts for different universities with different rules and regulations. This has stood in the way of co-ordination and even academic collaboration. The Council, therefore, decided to set up a Committee, under the Chairmanship of Chandrasekharan Pillai, Director, National Judicial Academy, to draft a model Act, which could be adopted by all the universities with minor changes, if necessary.

The Committee examined the various enactments under which the universities in Kerala were established. The Committee felt that there should be one model enactment. Accordingly, a Draft Bill was prepared with the following major recommendations:

- With a view to giving due importance to academic freedom and autonomy to universities, the administrative bodies should be constituted by academicians to insulate the universities from un-academic political interferences that cripple the growth of quality in higher education.

- Appointments to faculty positions shall be made in accordance with relevant UGC regulations in the matter.
- Appointments to non-teaching positions, except those to statutory positions, shall be made by the Kerala Public Service Commission.
- There should be a University Appellate Tribunal in operation (at present, despite existence of provisions, they are not in effective operation in the universities).
- The local fund audit in the Government of Kerala should not have any jurisdiction with reference to the university funds. Instead, each university should have its own audit wing, which shall be responsible to the Government directly and through the Accountant General. Alternatively, there could be a common audit organisation for all the universities in Kerala.
- The universities should exercise academic and administrative supervision over colleges and recognised institutions affiliated to the universities concerned vis-a-vis appointment of faculty and non-teaching staff and their service conditions including a uniform staff pattern and pay scales.
- All universities should have a common academic and examination calendar.
- To encourage excellence in teaching and research, Assistant Professors and Associate Professors, who secure externally funded projects with specific provisions for appointment of Associate Professor/Professor, may be appointed to the respective higher position during the tenure of the project, provided that such appointment shall not entail any additional financial liability to the university.

- The current practice of following different laws on recruitment of staff etc. presents a disparate picture. The universities should be streamlined to achieve uniformity. Statutes should also be uniform to the extent possible.

The Committee faced a crisis when it came to determining the qualifications of Vice Chancellors. The Chairman and another member of the Committee were of the view that the appointment of Vice Chancellors should be strictly in accordance with the regulations of the UGC. But a majority of the members, some of whom had vested interests, insisted on not prescribing any specific qualification in terms of teaching experience. The Committee, therefore, submitted a report with a majority and minority opinion, and the Chairman himself was with the minority.

I explained in the Foreword to the Report submitted to the Government that the submission of the Report was delayed because the Committee had difference of opinion on some of the recommendations of the Report. The Executive Council of the KSHEC took some time to reconcile the differences and to prepare a comprehensive set of recommendations.

In effect, the compromise formula suggested by the Council became meaningless. It states that 'the Vice Chancellor should be a person with the highest level of competence, integrity, morals and institutional commitment. The only other requirement is that he should not be above the age of 65 at the time of consideration.' The weakness of the whole Report was the vague and unspecified qualifications of Vice Chancellors.

The Report was submitted to the Education Minister, but no action was taken on the report.

Chapter 16

IT@COLLEGES

Having identified the use of technology as an urgent requirement for higher education reform, the Executive Council of the KSHEC held extensive discussions with the stakeholders on upgrading the IT equipment and other facilities relating to technology.

The functions and responsibilities of the KSHEC include evolving 'new concepts and programmes in higher education.' Quality in higher education derives from the quality of infrastructure (laboratories, library, classrooms, amenities), curriculum, pedagogy, assessment and evaluation, and the quality and commitment of the personnel (teachers, administrators, facilitators and management). To deliver quality undergraduate and postgraduate education, which will provide the students the edge in the competitive employment market, it is necessary that all elements of college and university-level learning and teaching ecosystem embrace the best of today's educational technology and practices. As educationists worldwide have discovered, and indeed endorsed, Information Technology provides some of the best tools and solutions to make this happen.

Kerala leads the nation when it comes to indices of literacy and quality of life of her people. Colleges and universities need to be focused on making sure that students are ready for the careers that await them when they graduate and enter the workforce. KSHEC believes that Kerala students deserve, and indeed demand, our best efforts to make this happen.

The KSHEC constituted a Committee named 'IT @ Colleges Committee' in July 2013 with experts in the IT field to study the available IT facilities in the colleges in Kerala and also to ensure that every college in Kerala has the required infrastructure for the use of technology for teaching and to develop content for the courses. I chaired the Committee, not because of any expertise in the matter, but to indicate the importance of technology. We had, among various experts, Anand Parthasarathy, a veteran technologist who had directed several IT initiatives in Kerala.

The Report of the Committee gave a brief idea about the current developments in the field of Information Technology and how we can make use of those facilities in the colleges in Kerala. The field of higher education in Kerala can be improved by introducing e-learning facilities such as Smart Classrooms, Virtual Labs, Massive Open Online Courses (MOOCs), etc. The Report also examined the IT facilities introduced by the Government of Kerala in the colleges in Kerala. The opportunities and the challenges faced by the Government to implement e-learning were also covered.

The details of the study conducted by KSHEC about the current availability of systems and equipment in Government and aided colleges in Kerala was also included in the Report. Based on the study, a cost estimate was prepared by KSHEC to implement a Technology Enhanced Learning and Teaching (TELT) facility at colleges.

The experts did a thorough study of the available IT resources and the minimum enhancement of such resources to attain efficiency and to transform the present situation. The cost of an optimum arrangement was calculated at Rs 103.7 lakh for five years for each college. To support 199 colleges that indicated interest, the requirement for five years was Rs 206.36 crore.

Although the cost envisaged was reasonable and the need was urgent, the Government took no action on the Report. IT equipment is being purchased on an ad hoc basis without any framework and guidelines. I have tried to probe the colleges about the equipment in their possession, but the facilities were confined to the computer labs in the colleges and most students had no access to the computers and the internet.

Chapter 17

INCENTIVES FOR TEACHERS

The present higher education system in the State does not have a system of providing incentives for meritorious and performing teachers. The continued absence of any incentives for performance might lead to either complacency or even de-motivation in the performing individuals. Therefore, there is a need to assess the performance of teachers and link it with incentives in the form of recognition and rewards. Hence, the KSHEC appointed a Committee to study the feasibility of granting incentives to teachers. The objectives were to establish a mechanism for objective assessment of teachers in higher education and for linking performance with rewards to recognise and felicitate teachers in higher education on the basis of their performance according to various criteria such as teaching, research, extension and innovative practices, and thereby incentivising their performance.

The Committee accepted my suggestion that the most important incentive, which could be given to the best teachers, is the creation of a separate cadre for them. The proposal for the formation of an All India Service, designated as the Indian Education Service has been lying dormant. The Committee recommended that this may be revived to create a cadre of professional educationists to shoulder high responsibilities, both academic and administrative.

The Committee devised various categories of awards for principals, and senior and young teachers at the university and college levels. Some innovative awards, for example, a special research award, were suggested. Specific criteria and the selection process were also laid down.

After submitting the report, the Council sought authorisation from the Government to start the process of selection, but there was no response from the Government, obviously not because of any objection, but because of mere lethargy and neglect.

Chapter 18

LIBERALISATION OF ACADEMIC TRAVEL

Mobility of teachers and students is an essential part of good modern education. For centuries, Indian scholars have been travelling abroad and receiving scholars from other countries. Ironically, academic travel has become more and more restricted for various reasons. Fears about foreign interference, terrorism, corruption and brain drain are the possible reasons for these restrictions.

Any research activity in the fields of science, technology, arts and humanities needs the acquisition of state-of-the-art knowledge and familiarisation with the practices in the respective fields. One of the ways to share the continuously developing knowledge is participation in international seminars, conferences, workshops, etc. Academicians and scholars in the respective fields from across the world are all brought to a common platform, where healthy exchange of ideas and sharing of experiences and expertise takes place. Thus, participation in international conferences and workshops is essential for acquiring and maintaining high standards of academic excellence and doing research of global relevance. Further, there is scope for collaborative research projects that might enable the exchange of scholars between India and other countries, with a two-way value addition of the knowledge gained.

Presently, all Government officials including university and college teachers should get prior permission from the State Government and Central Home Department before making such travel. In the normal course, for international conferences, the acceptance letter and invitation letter are received at the most two months before the commencement of the programme, which is often too short a period for obtaining sanction of the State Government. As per the present guideline, the Government approval requires various time-consuming procedures.

This issue of procedural delay was discussed at the International Relations Group of the Department of Higher Education and it was decided that the Council should constitute a group to frame recommendations for consideration by the Government. Accordingly, the KSHEC constituted a Committee to frame recommendations for consideration of the Government under the Chairmanship of K Mohandas IAS (Rtd) and with R Jayaprakash as the Convener.

The Committee held six meetings and invited the Heads of various departments and representatives of teachers' organisations and other stakeholders for interaction. The Committee made some efforts to obtain information on the number of teachers deputed abroad for training and the nature of programmes which they attended, but did not have the benefit of getting the data.

The Committee came to the conclusion that academic travel should be treated differently from the travel of Government officials, who travel for official business. A whole set of recommendations, based on the need for speedy decisions for academic travel, ready availability of funding, either national or international, and the extreme importance of familiarity with latest technologies. Safeguards were built into these recommendations to ensure that there is no misuse.

We were aware that liberalisation of academic travel was not within the purview of the State Government, but it was necessary for the Government to frame proposals for the ministries of Human Resource Development, Home Affairs and External Affairs. No such initiative was taken by the Department of Higher Education.

Chapter 19

RESEARCH: THE RIGHT WAY

The sorry state of affairs of research in our universities is too well known to be elaborated here. The whole purpose of research is to secure a degree to fulfil the requirement for certain jobs. But research degrees are so common today that it does not amount to much in the job market. But more sadly, research is for mere information gathering and not for creating new knowledge. No Nobel Laureate has emerged from our university system and even patents are very rare. Facilities for research are extremely poor and successive guides perpetuate the mediocre system. The way research guides exploit their research wards in various ways is a scandal. The lowest point was reached when no action was taken on a Pro-Vice Chancellor who was found guilty of plagiarising 63 per cent of his thesis. I had tried to generate some debate on the subject by speaking and writing about it. No one took notice.

A discussion I had with some of the Professors in Calicut university threw up the idea of doing a study on the state of research in the universities with particular reference to facilities for research. The study was entrusted to a group of eminent scholars, headed by Gangan Prathap. He went beyond the immediate task of improving research facilities and went into the system of research itself. Several sub-committees were formed for different subjects. The Report came towards the end of the term of the Executive Council. The report could not be considered in depth, but it is an excellent one, which ought to be studied and implemented if the level of our research work is to be upgraded.

Chapter 20

HIGHER EDUCATION FOR THE FUTURE: A JOURNAL FOR THE COUNCIL

The credit of thinking about a Journal for the Council should go to my predecessor, Panicker, but he did not take the proposal forward, except for getting together an International Advisory Board. He had initiated some discussions with Sage Publications, but they remained inconclusive. I picked up the idea where Panicker had left off and actually brought out the first issue of the Journal, 'Higher Education for the Future' at the time of the International Meet on Transnational Education in 2014.

Sage Publications were co-operative and an Editorial Board put together under me worked extremely well. Contributions came from different parts of the Globe and we had much to choose from. We maintained a balance between the contributions from the State, the rest of India and abroad. Though the quality of production and substance were of a high standard, marketing was difficult. Since subscription was low, the Council had to fund most of the production costs. I found that there were more contributors than readers. Peer review was a challenge as there were not enough volunteers to do the review competently.

A by-product of the Journal was a series of workshops, we conducted for potential contributors. This was a success as many teachers were keen to acquire skills in writing, editing and publishing journals, essentially for career advancement.

The Journal is a very important instrument for exchange of ideas and to keep in touch with the trends in higher education around the Globe. But not much use is being made of international experience as we are caught in our own mindset, which is not conducive to change.

Chapter 21

CLUSTERING OF COLLEGES

A brilliant idea created by the UGC, the formation of clusters of colleges to share academic resources in certain areas, did not succeed because of the characteristic lack of trust and suspicion of anything new. My predecessor formed three clusters in different cities, but they were boycotted by the aided colleges for fear that close interaction and physical mobility of students and teachers would be against their interests. Only the government colleges joined the scheme and the grants given to cluster activities were spent without benefit to all the members.

I decided to make an effort to entice the aided colleges to join the scheme by changing the rules of the game to suit the convenience of the aided colleges. More than a year was spent in the negotiations. We reached an agreement that the colleges in the cluster will not share resources with each other, but will organise chosen group activities such as lectures, sports, cultural activities, etc. Clear rules were framed for such activities, to be funded by the Government. But quite unexpectedly, the aided colleges decided not to join the clusters.

We finally decided that the three clusters in Thiruvananthapuram, Ernakulam and Kozhikode would be energised. The only aided college which joined the cluster was the Cochin College. Different activities were designed for different clusters. Several courses for skilled development were started for the students of the clusters, but most courses were taken only by those who were in the colleges which hosted them. Laboratory equipment was set up in one of the colleges and yoga equipment was supplied to one of the colleges, which was made available to others.

The most innovative scheme was a video link, which was established in the Ernakulam cluster, with connectivity to the Council. Lectures given in one of the colleges could be of benefit to all the colleges of the cluster. The equipment for the video link was procured through Keltron, which turned out to be totally inefficient and probably corrupt. The prices quoted by the vendor were hiked and the specifications were tampered with. Consequently, we were supplied with low-quality equipment, which would not match. The vendors finally revealed to us the machinations of Keltron, but that was of no benefit to the project. The video link was established and a few lectures were delivered by eminent speakers on different subjects, but the enthusiasm waned very fast because of the poor quality of the images and the sound.

A bigger problem arose when a rumour was spread by someone that the video link was installed to reduce the number of teachers in different colleges. Within days, someone tampered with the whole system and rendered it unusable. It turned out that the old suspicion about technology replacing jobs is still there and it is difficult to change the mindset even in the 21st century. The reason for inadequate use of technology in higher education is this deep suspicion and the poor quality of the equipment supplied because of middlemen and corruption.

The whole idea of setting up of cluster of colleges was that such clusters will eventually become independent universities and thus move away from the affiliation system. But the move failed in Kerala because of the mindset of mistrust, of being suspicious of one another and the inability to co-ordinate. Principals considered it a burden to do extra work to administer the clusters. Frequent changes of Principals was also a hurdle to the operation of the clusters. In spite of all these hurdles, the Thiruvananthapuram cluster organised some special courses and also a sports meet.

Chapter 22

CABBAGES AND KINGS

The Council had several routine responsibilities, ranging from the administration of a scholarship scheme to running the Erudite Programme, organising monthly lectures and rendering advice to the Government on service and academic matters. The scholarship programme was to be funded initially by the Government and to be moved to voluntary contributions and endowments. Appeals for funds did not elicit much of a response and even a pledge for annual support made by a voluntary organisation was withdrawn. In the circumstances, the scholarship was fully funded by the State Government. The administration of the scholarship was problematic because of the tardy approach by the colleges and lack of data about the performance of the scholars for continuation of the scholarships. But many students at the graduate and postgraduate levels benefited from the scheme.

The Erudite Programme was meant to bring high-level scholars, particularly Nobel Laureates, to the universities. But the programme was in disarray as funds were allotted in bulk and it was difficult to monitor the expenditure. The level of the scholars invited kept going down. The Council took over and administered the programme and insisted that the level of the scholars should be high and the expenditure low. We also insisted that scholars invited by one institution should be shared with others. There were a couple of allegations of misuse of the scheme to promote friends and, even worse, for making reciprocal deals with foreign scholars. These were curbed by the Council by taking over the administration of the Scheme. However, the Erudite Programme did not bring in the kind of benefit as was expected. The work involved in locating scholars, organising their lectures and getting the right audiences for them and taking care of them did not attract many takers.

Monthly lectures were easy to arrange, but finding an audience was a challenge. We had some eminent speakers, but not much enthusiasm by the targeted audiences. The calendars of the institutions are very crowded and it is very hard to extricate some time for such activities.

The mechanism devised for the Council to give advice on service and academic matters was used to delay action or to shift responsibility. The decisions in which the Department was interested were taken without any reference to the Council, but others were thrown into the lap of the Council. We were never informed of the final decision taken on any issue on which we rendered advice.

An International Relations Group (IRG) was set up by the Department of Higher Education. Its responsibility was to find solutions to the various challenges faced by the universities in foreign collaboration with respect to transfer of credit, schedule of examinations, capacity issues, fee sharing, student visa, entry examination equivalency, faculty shortage, modern courses, selection criteria and administrative delay. The Group was coordinated jointly by the Vice Chairman, KSHEC, and the Principal Secretary, Department of Higher Education. Two representatives each from the University of Kerala, MG University, University of Calicut, Kannur University and CUSAT were nominated to the Group. Financial assistance for enhancing international relations by way of preparing brochures was sanctioned by the Council to the University of Kerala, MG University, University of Calicut and Kannur University. Except Calicut University, all other universities prepared international brochure and submitted them to the Government. The Group authorised the universities to disseminate the brochures widely, but nothing was done to attract foreign students.

Another project initiated by the Group was the construction of special international hostels in each university. Proposals for financial assistance for construction of hostel with special facilities for international students, were submitted by various universities and forwarded to the Department of Higher Education for further necessary action. The universities were asked to prepare a common design and budget, but no action appears to have been taken. The new Council will, hopefully, pursue the proposal and obtain the requisite financial sanction.

I travelled to all the universities in Kerala and many colleges, making use of the invitations received to participate in academic events. I was astonished how the allocations made by various sources for academic activities were being spent on rituals, ceremonies and feasting. A typical national or international seminar begins with a formal opening to which, apart from the main speaker, many local dignitaries are invited. Most of them have no knowledge of the topic under discussion, but they hold forth interminably, taking away the precious time of the seminar. Money is spent on flowers covered with plastic and souvenirs made of plastic, wood or glass for the dignitaries and entertainment. By the time the first business session begins, the delegates are exhausted by the speeches and entertainment.

Early in my term, I advised all the institutions, who sought financial support from the Council for academic events, to avoid rituals and unnecessary expenditure. I specifically requested that flex boards, flowers and souvenirs should be avoided. But sheer habit and custom compelled them to continue these practices and I myself ended up with a vast collection of souvenirs of various kinds, which remain as symbols of the problems of higher education in Kerala, such as resistance to change, lack of clear objectives, faith in established practices and rituals, and wasteful expenditure.

ANNEXURES

ANNEX 1

Inaugural Address at the First Session of the Executive Council

(2 November 2011)

I am delighted to congratulate you on your appointment as the members of the Executive Council of the Kerala State Higher Education Council. I look forward to working with you to enhance the value and prestige of higher education in Kerala.

You have brought to the Council a wealth of experience in the field of education. Each one of you has been chosen for your eminence and wisdom. I have myself spent much of my working life in diplomacy, but my heart has been in education. With both my parents as school teachers, I have grown up in the midst of the joys and tears of educating young minds. I began my career as a teacher and even after I returned to India after 37 years abroad, I found immense satisfaction in teaching in several universities in India and outside. I was pleasantly surprised when I was offered this position, previously occupied by a veteran educationist.

Education and diplomacy have much in common. Unlike the other civil services, the Foreign Service has very few files and it demands constant education as we change countries and continents every three years. The challenge to cope with a new country, a new civilization, a new language and a new system can be met only by remaining a student throughout. Reading, research and writing are as essential for diplomats as for academics. Perhaps this is the reason why several distinguished diplomats, among them Sardar KM Panikkar, Shri G. Parthasarathy, Shri KR Narayanan and Shri Hamid Ansari, were appointed as Vice-Chancellors. Shri KPS Menon (Sr) has recorded that he was offered the Vice-Chancellorship of several universities when he returned from Moscow. I welcome this opportunity to bring to this position my exposure to the world and my zest for igniting the young minds, in the words of former President Abdul Kalam.

Allow me to pay a tribute to my predecessor, Dr KN Panikkar, and his team for building up this Council from its very beginning and for laying the foundations for making higher education in Kerala purposeful and relevant to the demands of modern times. They have introduced several reforms and suggested many more, with the help of other experts. Our first task is to give attention to these reforms and promote their implementation after critically examining them in the light of past experience and applying the correctives as necessary. The scholarships scheme, the clustering of colleges, the Erudite Scheme, combating of ragging in the campuses, the Teacher Exchange Programme, the publication of a Journal, etc. have broad acceptance and must be pursued vigorously. The reforms on which there may be difference of opinion in the academic community should be examined with the realization that the pursuit of perfection should not endanger the existing good. The advice we give to the Government on policy formulation should be well considered; they should reflect the consensus in the academic community and they should be practical and beneficial. Effective monitoring of the programmes and utilization of funds must be one of our important functions.

The general approach I would recommend is one of continuity and change. As a student in Kerala, I was often bewildered by frequent changes in the education system. We should not subject our student community to needless experimentation and change. Our purpose should be to fashion an education system that will meet the challenges of the future. Swami Vivekananda used to say that the end of all education is 'man making.' Education is 'the manifestation of the perfection already in man,' he observed. Education, for him, means that process by which character is formed, strength of mind is increased and intellect is sharpened, as a result of which one can stand on one's feet.

The lofty ideals of a broad education that will elevate the society must be upheld, but after everything is said and done, our education system will be judged by the extent to which it equips our youth to compete nationally and globally for careers. We have had a long tradition of seeking fortunes abroad and the fact that many have succeeded in building successful careers abroad is a compliment to our education system, however inadequate it is perceived to be. We should, therefore, keep an eye on the opportunities worldwide and fashion courses that will suit the needs in different countries. The system should be flexible enough to introduce courses at short notice to cater to urgent demands. Even while stressing the importance of the study of Indian languages, proficiency in the English language must be given high priority to make our graduates able to compete in the international markets. Study of international relations should also be expanded with the same objective. Needless to say, education should inculcate not only our values and culture, but also the civic sense of our citizens to make them valuable members of the society.

I hope the reconstituted Council will be thoughtful, innovative and fast in devising new schemes to bring about the necessary changes in higher education. There is no dearth of studies, reports and recommendations to choose from. But more important is the implementation of decisions in a highly complex system. We should be conscious that there is no level playing field for our academic community. While the variety of different managing and financing systems will remain, it should be possible for every institution to give equal opportunities to the academic community. The role of the Council should be to create a level playing field for higher education in Kerala. We can secure the co-operation of the multitude of agencies and administrations, whether in the Government or the private sector, only if we demonstrate professionalism, transparency and care, the very principles that the present Government of Kerala espouses.

Ideally, we should strive to elevate every institution to a level of excellence, but given the history, the availability of resources and the existing variations in standards, it is inevitable that this should be accomplished in stages. I am happy to know that the Centre has already agreed, in principle, to establish an IIT in Kerala in the 12th Plan. We, as the Council, should advise the Government of Kerala to take the necessary steps to establish an IIT in Kerala as soon as possible. Similarly, the proposed Malayalam University and Open University should be established as soon as possible. We already have institutions of repute in Kerala. I would suggest that we devise a scheme by which a number of these institutions are selected for intensive efforts to turn them into institutions of excellence. We might begin with a rating mechanism for colleges so that improvement can be noted and incentives given to deserving institutions. The selection can be made from the colleges that volunteer to join the scheme. One element of the scheme will be the linking up of these entities with national and international institutions of excellence. If the Council accepts this scheme, it should be submitted to the Government before the end of the year.

We are required to prepare our programme for the 12th Plan in a matter of days. This requires urgent thinking on what we can accomplish in higher education in the next five years. Nationally, this is a time for introspection and self-appraisal to see whether we can usher in an era of high-quality teaching and research. We read with consternation recently that a country which attracted knowledge seekers from around the Globe to Nalanda and Takshila does not have a single university to find a place in international ranking. Shri JAK Tareen, the Vice-Chancellor of the Pondicherry University, has identified three major differences between Indian universities and well-known world class universities, which prevent us from attaining excellence. 'First, Indian universities and colleges totally lack in critical mass of students. Secondly, the undergraduate programmes are fragmented from the university campuses, and, thirdly, the existing affiliation system of colleges to universities is the bottleneck of their autonomy and freedom to grow with innovations. These issues need to be addressed for our universities to attain global parity, though other issues of faculty, infrastructure, laboratories, library and a conducive ambience are as important,' he states. We shall have to meet again shortly to suggest measures to be included in the 12th Plan to meet our aspiration to create a knowledge society.

I would emphasize the need for the broadest possible consultations with the stakeholders on a continuing basis. In this, I would solicit the participation of all members of the Council. I shall begin consultations on a regular basis with groups and individuals from next week and I would urge you also to do so in designated constituencies. We should visit as many institutions as possible within a short time to get new ideas and thoughts. We should increase our interaction with the universities in the rest of India and abroad. We do not claim monopoly over wisdom and we hope to gain our insights from the continuous interaction with the academic community.

The message that should go from this first meeting of the Council is that KSHEC will work with the clear purpose of making a difference to higher education in Kerala to enable our youth to meet the challenges of the present and the future. We shall do this without fear or favour, affection or ill will and we expect, in turn, the full cooperation, support and goodwill from the entire academic community and the public at large. The doors of the Council will remain open for ideas, suggestions and recommendations and I invite the public to interact freely with me and the members of the Council.

I wish you the very best as we embark on a journey together. I have great pleasure and honour to inaugurate the first meeting of the Executive Council.

ANNEX 2

Inaugural Address of Kalpatha 2011
By Former Ambassador TP Sreenivasan, Vice-Chairman, KSHEC, at Technopark

(19 November 2011)

Thank you for inviting me to inaugurate Kalpatha 2011, a two-day national conference on the topic of 'Business Innovation: The New Age Survival Mantra.' You have invited me at a time when I am in the process of reinventing myself. To put it in computer terminology, I am struggling to put new software into the hardware that is accustomed to a different set of circumstances and demands. After being an evangelist of foreign policy and strategic thinking, I have now moved to the academic world, with a mandate to help the Kerala Government formulate its policy on higher education. My only consolation is that there have been several diplomats before me, who made the switch and done as well in academics as in diplomacy. In a way, my own appointment as the Executive Head of the KSHEC is an innovation on the part of the Government of Kerala.

I have agreed to speak here today not because I have much to say about innovation, which is now a vast subject for discussion in the business world. I am fascinated by your commitment to uphold the recent trends and issues in management and bridge the gap between the corporate world and academia. In fact, the first new topic that my Council adopted for implementation was the Institution-Industry Interface, a programme of close interaction between educational institutions and the industry.

The nature of interaction between educational institutions and industry has changed significantly over the years in India. In the colonial era, there was little interaction between the two, as the university system essentially supplied human capital to staff the civil service and judiciary. It was not purported to cater to the industrial workforce. Post-independence, graduates of Indian university system found employment in a much wider range of careers, including in industry. Other forms of university industry linkages, such as industry-sponsored research projects, joint publications, business incubators in universities, have started to flourish recently in certain institutions such as IITs and IISC. These institutions have witnessed higher intensity university industry linkages. For instance, all the business incubators started in academia in India can be traced to IITs and IISC. When IIT Kanpur was ranked as number one among engineering colleges, the reason was that it had received a high amount of alumni money in the form of university–industry linkages. This benefits the industry because they get young brains to work in their research and development programs and the university students get great exposure to the industry. For this very reason, these institutions are considered institutions of excellence and enjoy greater autonomy. My ambition is to create such institutions in Kerala.

It goes without saying that there is a strong connection between autonomy enjoyed by institutions like the IITs and the intensity with which it participates in the nation's innovative system. The Government funding for research, which is channeled through public research institutes has not been fully utilized for the purpose intended. For this reason, the Government now proposes to create innovation universities with greater autonomy in matters of academics, faculty, personnel, finance, administration, and in the development of a vision for the future. These universities will make our universities more active participants in the country's innovative system.

India's economic success story is based on growth in business services, including information technology services that are mainly non-patentable and do not require formal research and development (R&D) spending. This may appear comfortable in the short term, but to compete at the global level, research at the university level has to be an essential part of our strategy. Absence of research will make our graduates mere labour in the world markets. New streams of technology can be invented only when education endeavors to meet demand.

A UNESCO Policy Forum concluded in 2000 that one of the most important challenges for institutional policymakers is defining a legal framework and incentive systems which stimulate innovation at the institutional, departmental and individual levels. A balance has to be achieved between the culture and traditions of a university with existing outside opportunities for collaboration. Bringing these opportunities to the campuses is the objective of the Institutions–Industry Interface that the Executive Council is planning to accomplish.

Increasingly, industries are becoming the beneficiaries of the products of our universities and, therefore, they have a responsibility to invest in education, particularly research. We do not have major manufacturing industries in Kerala, but our graduates do work in other parts of India and abroad. Partnership with major industrial houses will benefit both the universities and the industries. Needless to say, the knowledge industry, which is growing in Kerala has even a greater stake in education and research.

Coming back to innovation in its present sense of invention and renovation, interestingly, the most innovative companies such as Google, Facebook, Twitter, etc. do not claim to be innovative, while those who are still trying to be innovative speak of the importance of innovation. Those who have acquired game-changing technologies go beyond innovation; they create revolutions. Steve Jobs and Mark Zuckerberg are not innovators, but visionaries, to borrow a word from an earlier era. Innovation may well be for lesser mortals, but innovation is essential for business and it is the survival mantra of today.

Innovation is traditionally measured by the number of patents a company files, but more recently there is a tendency to measure it in terms of influence and global reach. The result is a list of 100 most innovative companies in the world and the surprise is that not a single Chinese company is on the list. Yet, China has become the most prolific patent filer in the world, pursuing a national plan to become an economy based on innovation rather than imitation. The Chinese plan calls for its corporations and individual investors to file two million patents by 2015, which would dwarf the current filing in the US. The absence of Chinese firms on the list of innovators has been attributed to focusing on the domestic market first.

But it will not be long before the Chinese secure global reach and become one of the most innovative countries. Like in other areas of business, China is ahead of us in patents and it is poised to compete with the US.

In education, however, vision is more important than innovation. However, in the short term, innovative ideas are as important in education as in business. The search for answers is the essence of education, just as business today cannot prosper without constant search for new applications of old inventions, if not new inventions and discoveries. In the laboratories, failures are not uncommon and success comes only after repeated failures, while in education, failures can do lasting damage. But in education as well as in business, tireless efforts are essential for new concepts and new applications, in other words, innovation.

I would like to conclude with what Leonardo da Vinci had to say about the vital importance of inquisitiveness in life. 'I roamed the countryside searching for answers to things I did not understand. Why shells existed on the top of mountains along with imprints of coral and plant and seaweed are usually found in the sea? Why the thunder lasts a longer time than that which causes it? Why immediately on its creation the lightning becomes visible to the eye, while thunder takes time to travel? How the various circles of water form around the spot which has been struck by a stone and why a bird sustains itself in the air? These questions and other strange phenomena engaged my thought throughout my life.' Some of the phenomena that bewildered Leonardo have been explained by science, but others remain. Both business and education must be constantly in search for answers to these questions, leading to innovation and vision.

ANNEX 3

Quality in Higher Education and Research: Par with International Standards

Address to the Conference of Vice-Chancellors, Kochi

(16 December 2012)

I am grateful to the Vice-Chancellor of Cochin University and the Association of Indian Universities (AIU) for inviting me to participate in this conference of the top educationists of India. I was delighted also to hear an inspiring address by the Chairman of the University Grants Commission.

Diplomacy, they say, is so important that it cannot be left to the diplomats alone. Similarly, education too is too important to be left to educationists alone. Perhaps, it is for this reason that I have been asked to head the Kerala State Higher Education Council, which I represent at this conference. What encourages me is the fact that some good educationists have become good ambassadors and some good ambassadors have become good educationists in the past.

The theme of today's discussion on quality of higher education in India with reference to international standards will itself raise controversies. World-class education and international standards have been rejected by some sections of the Indian intelligentsia.

When I said at the Kannur University the other day that I was sad to know that none of our universities or IITs had figured in a list of world-class universities, I was told by an economist that he was not bothered about such lists, which made odious comparisons. He would prefer to have our own system of education, focusing on our culture and traditions. To my observation that my endeavour is to make our graduates competitive nationally and internationally, he said that the purpose of education was to create 'organic intellectuals.' I would not go into that debate now. I would merely examine whether some of the methods used in other countries can be helpful to us in improving our own standards.

If the objective of giving world-class education to our students is accepted, international standards and systems of education must be studied and an effort should be made to adopt the best practices, wherever they are found. I would bring some of these to your attention and discuss how we can adopt them for our own needs.

We claim that we have succeeded in enhancing quantity, if not quality, in education, but the fact of the matter is that our gross enrollment ratio is only 15% and we are planning to increase it to 30% by 2020. This would mean 30 million students more, 1000 universities more, 50,000 colleges more and one million teachers more, as pointed out by our HRD Minister at the recent Washington summit. The Foreign Education Bill, when enacted, will facilitate entry of foreign universities, but such universities will not be able to repatriate profits. They would, however, benefit from their exposure to Indian academic life, it was stated. Secretary of State, Hillary Clinton, pointed out that there was a wide gap between India's needs and what the USA can do. But we can certainly benefit from some of the reforms introduced in other countries.

Developing countries are generally resistant to Western concepts for fear that they will impose cultural, political and economic priorities of imperialism. Ideological crystallization has led to reaffirmation of the sovereignty of States and the belief that quality has been colonized by consumerism and commoditization of education.

Quality evaluation and assessment are fairly new features of education in Europe and the United States. Till 1990, it was believed that quality was implicit in university education, but gradually, the concept of external evaluation came to be accepted. As a result, external examination system was introduced in the UK, the USA adopted a system of accreditation, and Ministerial control of education became fashionable in much of Europe. With massification, internationalization and marketization of education, it became necessary to evaluate higher education despite calls for autonomy of universities. India adopted the assessment and accreditation system in recent years and NAAC has been a success in aiming at excellence and equity-driven growth in higher education. Following this example, the Kerala State Higher Education Council has decided to explore the possibility of setting up a state assessment machinery to continuously assess institutions and teachers, with a view to providing them incentives for better performance.

Professionalization of education is another feature that we can emulate from the Western world. Students are diverted to professions early in life. The community colleges in the USA provide models for training and retraining the work force and creating employment opportunities.

Academic freedom, autonomy and accountability are well defined in Western education. Academic freedom is universal and absolute, while autonomy is parochial and relative. Universities are accountable to a variety of clients, in addition to the Governments. They are accountable to the students, the parents and the business community. We must remove intellectual fetters from the universities, but hold them accountable to the society. Autonomy should not be used to undermine accountability.

Emphasis on research, even at the undergraduate level, is another feature of Western education we should emulate. Research can play a central role in promoting informed deliberations. Research remains abysmally low in India even at the graduate level and this needs to be changed in accordance with international standards.

Frequent changes in curriculum to reflect the changes in society is a feature of Western education. In fact, changes in curriculum become forces for social change in certain circumstances. In the USA, the curriculum swings from tradition and conservatism to experimentation and growth as social movements become the key motivator for curricular change. In our system, curricular changes are few and far between. A dynamic curriculum should be the hallmark of any vibrant education system.

Education in many countries need to cope with increasing diversity in terms of race, ethnicity, gender, class, religion, sexual orientation, gender identity and disability. Higher education has a role in achieving the promise of democracy and a pluralistic society. In India, diversity is a reality that has been taken into account in educational reform. Some of the experiments in other countries to cope with diversity by prescribing different methodologies may be relevant to our own higher education.

My point is not that our quest for quality in higher education should be guided only by international practices and standards. We should suit our own genius and circumstances in fashioning a system of our own. My effort was just to point out certain features of external experiences, which may be relevant to our reform efforts.

ANNEX 4

India IT Summit Thiruvananthapuram

(19 January 2012)

Preparedness to Meet the Challenges

The challenges faced by the IT industry in India and the rest of the world are literally at our finger tips. A Google search will bring up any number of lists of top challenges, compiled by IT professionals, managers, executives and academics. These range from global competition, deceleration of demand and inadequate productivity to lack of innovation and cultural incompatibility. There is no dearth of solutions either. This summit itself has thrown up ideas, which can be imaginatively implemented by our IT community, which is second to none in the world.

At a similar conference last year, I spoke of the transformation that the IT revolution has brought about in traditional professions, particularly diplomacy. In the last three months, my focus has shifted to higher education in Kerala, of which IT is an essential component. We consider ourselves the software super power of the world, but the sad fact is that our education system is not using even a fraction of the immense possibilities that the IT revolution has opened up. We live in two different worlds, one, which provides the best services to the world and the other, which still uses a stencil and poor ink to prepare important documents and to record research findings. Many educational institutions have no connectivity or technical capability to put IT to productive use. No database exists as to which institutions have the necessary equipment and training to cope with the challenges of technology or to create IT professionals with the required levels of skills, imagination and innovation. Like Macaulay's education system created clerks for the British Empire, we are producing the work force for the Microsoft and Apple empires. We have embellished the discoveries of others, but we still have not developed our own rival systems to conquer the IT world.

There are several aspects to bridging the huge gap between our universities and the IT world. One is to use IT as a tool for modern methods of education, such as teleconferencing, clustering and other interaction through the Internet. Computers in the universities must come alive and not just be used as hat stands or coffee tables. The cost of providing connectivity to every student is a financial and logistical challenge. The fast progress in technology will render equipment obsolete before it is installed. But a beginning has to be made. Second is the need for invention and innovation to move to the laboratories in the universities. Young minds engaged in research are the catalysts of innovation. An idea and a personal computer (PC) have combined to conquer cyberspace in garages in San Jose. Research has to be at the centre of higher education. The third need is for the IT industry to be deeply involved in planning research and learning to create graduates, who are competitive in the industry in Kerala, the rest of India and the world at large. The universities must provide guidance to the industry for investment, create products and processes and also create a competent workforce. The Higher Education Council has taken the initiative to create a forum for partnership between the industry and the universities. I invite you to participate in it to benefit both the industry and the academic world.

The IT industry and the education system must also find answers to the immense social problems that the IT revolution has generated. As Pico Iyer said in a *New York Times* article recently, 'the IT revolution came without an instruction manual.' It came like a tempest and shook the political, social and cultural foundations of the world. Before we realized it, we found ourselves in a new world, where information and knowledge came to us at lightning speed. A bewildered world is looking for an anchor to stabilize themselves. Unless the industry and the society shape the new world with care, the young generation will be blown away by the challenges of the information age, which is also known as technoculture and technocapitalism age. The opportunities are many, but the challenges are even more. Disparities in the traditional society in terms of national income, health care and education have increased substantially.

The bewildering flow of information requires a new approach to learning. What is really required is the skill to decide what to look for, how to retrieve it, how to process it, and how to use it for the specific task that prompted the search for information. The guidance that the parents gave in an earlier era has disappeared because they are considered illiterate in the digital age. The loss of the position of elders as wiser than the younger generation is the biggest consequence of the IT revolution. The young have suddenly become wiser than the old. The young have moved from knowing nothing about the world to knowing too much overnight.

The total reversal of the traditional configuration of the wise old men and the innocent young has transformed the role of the elders in society. The children and the grandchildren have become the source of information as they have access to the Internet. Disinformation and propaganda on the net is believed as the gospel truth. Someone created a spurious website on the 'Attitude of Cats and Bearded Men' with pseudo statistics only to find that it became part of animal behavior science! The digital revolution is opening doors to increased communication and involvement, but other doors are closing in front of the younger generation. Sadly, the younger generation is not aware that they are losing out in the new dispensation.

Today, communications between parents and children are through the sms or chat, depriving such communications the warmth of personal interaction. Husbands and wives send net messages to each other from the same bed. Body language and smiles that determine the quality of relationship have receded into the background. Cellphone based interaction between children and parents and husbands and wives tends to diminish the importance of personal interaction, robbing them of the opportunity to develop a well-defined sense of self that generally evolves through such interaction.

The dream of every youngster in our schools and colleges to reach the Silicon Valleys of the globe presents its own challenges. If the brightest and the best go to the IT industry, who will be left to become our doctors, our administrators, our politicians, our singers, dancers and artists? The IT professionals, consisting of our best minds, confine themselves to a single sector, leaving the rest of the arena to people with less talent. Would this be conducive to our growth as a developed country? We need good people for IT, but we need equally good people for every other field of activity. This is a challenge that the IT sector seems unaware of in its rush to grab the best brains. The universities should play a role by channelizing our brilliant minds to different sectors in equal measure and the IT should work with the universities to facilitate equity and justice in deploying our youngsters in all vital sectors. The future of IT itself will depend on well-managed development.

The information revolution has brought in speed into our lives, but speed, by itself, does not enhance quality of life. Henry David Thoreau said, 'the man whose horse trots a mile a minute does not carry the most important messages.' Many of you may recall the telling photograph of a rocket being carried to the launching pad by a bullock cart. Speed on the ground is unnecessary for the rocket to gain speed when it is launched. When things come at you very fast, you naturally lose touch with yourself, it has been said. To go back to Pico Iyer, when we have more and more ways to communicate, we will have less and less to say. In our bid to beat deadlines again and again, we lose lifelines, he said.

I am afraid I have strayed away from the challenges faced by IT to the challenges faced by the society on account of the information revolution. But these are the two sides of the same coin and one cannot be dealt with without dealing with the other. We should use the immense opportunities presented by the IT revolution, but we should also meet the challenges posed by it. The screen, however accomplished, cannot give us the emotional and moral character and we need to learn what is essential, not what is available. Merely running away from connectivity by seeking out 'black-hole resorts' or 'Internetless' weeks, only to return to this busy information highway will not reshape the IT sector to the advantage of man. The man is superior to the machine and he should prevail in the end.

ANNEX 5

CII Conference on Innovation in Higher Education

(Kochi, 21 February 2012)

My association with the CII has been long and deep. It began with a 'Made in India' show in Nairobi in 1996, continued in multiple ways in Washington in the late 90s and more recently with the Pravasi Bharatiya Divas celebrations in India and abroad. It has also been on my mind in the context of the decision of the KSHEC to devise a mechanism by which the industry and higher education institutions in Kerala can work together to mutual benefit. I am grateful that CII has taken the initiative to organize this conference on innovation in higher education and that I have been invited to participate in it.

Innovation is a word that industry has bequeathed to us to mean the adoption of a new idea, a new method or a new device that creates a new dimension of performance. In higher education, it should mean successful exploitation of new ideas, a new way of doing things, a change that improves administrative or scholarly performance, a transformational experience based on a new way of thinking.

Interestingly, the recent debate on innovation has identified what are called 'mature enterprises,' which are institutions in which it is hard to innovate. They are increasingly risk-averse, at times self-satisfied and under fiscal pressures to maintain status quo. Education certainly falls in this category as it is averse to change; it has a certain sense of accomplishment and it is unduly expensive to bring in innovation. As a 'mature enterprise' by definition, it is hard to introduce innovation in the field of education.

One should readily concede that higher education in Kerala has had its accomplishments. It has catered to the changing demands by creating courses, institutions and modern methods of teaching. Facilities for professional courses have multiplied over the years and the quantitative needs for education have been largely met. The best graduates of our institutions have proved competitive outside the state and the country. Having come back to the field of education in Kerala after 40 years, I am truly impressed with our accomplishments within the constraints of resource crunch, extreme competition and politicization.

Whether we call it innovation, reform or upgradation, there is no doubt that higher education needs immediate attention. First and foremost, education must be an equalizer in any society. We are unable to provide a level playing field to all as the best education goes to the most paying, not the most deserving. The variation in the availability of infrastructure, by itself, imposes discrimination in the facilities available to different students. In speaking of reform, we cannot ignore the need for massive infusion of resources to provide the necessary infrastructure to all institutions, whether in the public or the private sector.

Quality enhancement necessarily demands improvement of the faculty across the board. The first requirement of retaining teachers in higher education has been met to the extent that the pay scales have been increased. But we still do not have any linkage between wages and productivity. Continuous assessment of productivity of the faculty is important and the necessary incentives and disincentives must be offered for acquiring new skills and adopting technology to meet the current needs. For this reason, the Higher Education Council proposes the establishment of a State Assessment and Accreditation Council.

Teaching methods in the higher education institutions have to be distinctly different from those used at lower levels. University education should encourage the spirit of enquiry and self-study rather than give them prepared lessons. Such an approach should lead to research, which should become the centre of post-graduate education. A total transformation in the relation between the teacher and the taught, the teacher and the researcher and the teacher and the technician must come about at the university level. The university faculty should be the engineers, the philosophers and architects of change.

In most developed countries, important knowledge creation takes place inside the universities, while here, the universities merely imbibe readymade knowledge and expect the industry to absorb their graduates without any inputs from the industry. The universities should be able to guide investments to the right destinations, create new products and processes and evaluate industrial applications of knowledge generated in the campuses. Educational institutions can be self-sustaining if it can generate surpluses from the technology it develops. Research efforts across institutions can cultivate excellence and avoid duplication. Our universities should not be content with reinventing the wheel. Research in universities should not be an excuse for idleness or a pastime between a degree and a profession. Here, the Council has established a Committee to devise methods for the industry and the universities to work together on research and curriculum.

University education should combine face-to-face learning with the use of technology as technology cuts costs by sharing assets among different institutions without travel. Universities with large campuses and a considerable student mass will also be economical if technology is appropriately deployed.

Integration of learning with work is another reform that we ought to develop. Applying knowledge is the best way to learn and the teachers themselves should become the best practitioners. Soft skills of collaboration, teamwork, entrepreneurship and communication are best learnt through practice. Moreover, earning while learning is more crucial in developing countries than in the developed ones.

From Plato's Academy of ancient Greece to online programmes today, educational institutions have been innovating and reforming themselves. They are under constant stress forced by boards, accrediting agencies and Governments, who demand transparency, accountability and tangible evidence of success. In the ultimate analysis, however, success depends on quality, excellence indicators and adoption of technology.

The KSHEC, entrusted as it is with policy reforms in higher education, stresses continuity and change as we have to build on the past accomplishments to shape a system that meets the needs of the future. Whether we call it innovation, reform or change, education should aim at the development of the various faculties of our students so that they may contribute their best towards the progress of the society.

ANNEX 6

Challenges in Higher Education

(All India Radio Talk, 8 March 2012)

Addressing the Kerala Legislative Assembly a few days ago, the Governor of Kerala, HE Shri HR Bharadwaj, stated: 'My Government recognizes that higher education is a powerful instrument of economic and social transformation and will aim to ensure quality education based on access, equity and excellence. My Government realizes the importance of regaining the primacy of our State in the field of higher education. The thrust of our Government will be on encouraging the setting up of world-class institutions and infrastructure in the state.'

Indeed, the challenge is to fashion an education system, which will provide access, ensure equity and maintain excellence. Today, none of the Indian universities figures in any list of a hundred or more world-class universities identified by different assessment agencies. The wide gap between our universities and world-class universities must be bridged so that our graduates can compete with their peers in India and abroad.

Higher education system in the State has succeeded in increasing quantity to meet the aspirations of the youth. The enrollment rate in Kerala is higher than the national average. No one needs to deny himself higher education for want of accessibility, though he may not get the course or college of his choice. Of late, even engineering colleges have vacancies. We have also risen to the occasion when it comes to offering new courses, including cutting-edge technologies in some colleges and universities. Compared to the situation when I was a student at Kerala University till 1966, now there is a world of difference in quantity, diversity and quality in higher education. Modern methods of teaching, including the use of technology, have been introduced. Internet connectivity has opened up a new world of knowledge. In other words, the system has much to claim credit for.

But Kerala seems to have lagged behind in competitiveness. This is evident from the fact that our graduates have only a small share of seats in specialized institutions in Kerala and outside, for which national competition is necessary. Similarly, the share of our graduates in the IT industry worldwide is low. We need to reform our higher education in such a way that it matches the highest standards in the world and makes our graduates competitive.

We should recognize that reform in the field of higher education would be slow and painful. Innovation gurus concede that it is hard to introduce innovation in the so-called 'mature enterprises' as innovations can be risky and expensive. Past successes can also be a disincentive. Higher education is in this category of enterprises. Any failed innovation may put a whole generation into jeopardy. The available teachers may not be well equipped to impart the new system of education. Introduction of reforms should be after due deliberation and preparation. Any wrong step can be costly.

Inadequate infrastructure, particularly in the Government institutions, is an immediate challenge. 'Low living and high thinking' may be a good dictum, but our educational institutions should have the minimum comforts and conveniences to enable the teachers and students to perform at the optimum level. The disparities among the facilities available should also be a matter of concern. Libraries, laboratories and other facilities need modernization and upgrading as new courses are introduced. Internet connectivity, which remains low, is also crucial in higher education. Massive infusion of funds is necessary to improve the infrastructural facilities.

Teachers are the backbone of any system of education. The better the teachers, the better the students. Much has been done to improve the wages of teachers, but the wages are not linked to performance and the security of service tends to make some of them lethargic. There should be a system of evaluation to provide incentives and disincentives to teachers. The strength of the faculty must also increase to give teachers time to learn more and take time off to reinvigorate themselves. They should also have enough time to evaluate answer books and interact with their students. The present teacher-student ratio does not meet the basic academic requirements. Teachers training programmes and exchange programmes must be developed.

The basic weakness of our higher education system is that teaching and learning methods continue unchanged from schools to postgraduate studies. Teachers are the sources of all knowledge and the students merely imbibe knowledge. In higher education, the initiative for learning should come from the students and the teachers should be guides, evaluators and motivators. The spirit of enquiry should be encouraged in planning the curriculum and prescribing textbooks. As HE the Governor stated, 'Our universities must not only impart knowledge, but also create knowledge through research and innovation. New products and processes must emerge from our campuses, giving the industry a stake in our education system.' Today, industry merely recruits graduates. Instead, they should invest in education and participate in its planning so that the graduates meet the requirements of the industry without sacrificing the basic academic standards and overall development of their personalities.

Fluency in English language, particularly its spoken variety, is lacking among our graduates and it militates against the acceptability of our graduates outside Kerala. Stress should be given to articulation of ideas in English as well as in the mother tongue and opportunities should be given to them to use the language in everyday life. A special effort to develop linguistic skills must be made.

The Government of India is in the process of enacting laws to facilitate and regulate the operation of foreign universities in India. Since profit-making is prohibited, only those universities that have an interest in Indian knowledge and talents will come to India. Kerala should equip itself for the advent of foreign universities by establishing links with some of them in advance in anticipation. Emulating the best practices in foreign education is the first step towards building world-class universities.

Continuous assessment of institutions and teachers is absolutely essential to determine the amount of autonomy that individual institutions should enjoy. Institutions of excellence can be developed in the state by identifying the potential of each institution. A State assessment and accreditation mechanism is being planned to meet this requirement.

Two reforms introduced in higher education recently have shown how problems develop in implementation of reforms, even when they are sound in objectives. The introduction of the semester system at the graduate level was long overdue in the State and it has proved valuable nationally and internationally. It aims at broader acquisition of knowledge, encourages the spirit of enquiry and transforms the relationship between the teachers and the students. It certainly increases the workload of the students and teachers, as the number of examinations multiplies. The system was introduced rather hastily and without consequential changes in the curricula and the student-teacher ratio. As a result, several anomalies have cropped up, raising the demand for a return to the old system, which would be a retrograde step. We are in the process of examining the problems through wide consultations among the stakeholders and close examination by experts. The semester system should stay, but with the necessary correctives to make it an instrument of improvement in higher education.

The other reform, which met a similar fate, was the introduction of a cluster of colleges, aimed at sharing of resources among the colleges in the same area. But it has not yet taken off because of the reluctance of the private colleges to share their assets. The scheme is being examined to remove the apprehensions of the reluctant managements.

Everyone agrees with Swami Vivekananda that the purpose of education is 'man making.' It should bring out the talents already inherent in every individual. Our own ancient system of education remains a guide and efforts are being made to revive the spirit of Nalanda and Takshasila. But in modern terms, man making will also include equipping the students with skills that will enable them to stand on their own two feet, another point that Swami Vivekananada had stressed. As the saint Narayana Guru emphasized, education must develop the hand, the head and the heart. The challenge of higher education is to devise a system that will meet the multiple needs of our youth to meet the challenges of a rapidly changing world. They should be equipped to seize the opportunities of globalization, without being swept away by its tumultuous impact.

ANNEX 7

Higher Education: Challenges of Globalization

(IIT Delhi, Education Conference)

Indian Institutes of Technology have come to be acknowledged as educational institutions of excellence, even though they may not be on every list of world-class institutions of learning. The Delhi IIT has a special place in the pantheon of the great educational institutions. It is, therefore, an honour to be invited to the Delhi IIT for an educational seminar. The honour is even more, considering that I have only recently strayed into education, having spent the last 40 years in the Indian Foreign Service.

The debate today is not on the merits and demerits of globalization or on whether the onset of globalization can be halted or delayed. Frenetic crowds going on the rampage at venues of global conferences are things of the past. Globalization has come to stay and the need of the hour is to maximize its opportunities and minimize its challenges. I believe, like the legendary professor of Columbia University, Jagdish Bhagawati, that globalization is not only inevitable but also desirable for human development. To those who say globalization must have a human face, his reply is that globalization already has a human face.

No human activity has remained unaffected by globalization and education is no exception. Internationalization of education is considered a consequence of globalization. But we must remember that internationalization of education took place before globalization and that education has contributed to the advent of globalization. Education has not shown great respect for juridical boundaries and higher education has always been more internationally open than most sectors because of its immersion in knowledge.

Globalization has been defined in many ways, but it is essentially 'the widening, deepening and speeding up of interconnectedness.' Fast communication is an essential feature of globalization, but internationalization of education took place when travel was still by sailboats and horses. Movement of people at that time depended on the wind in their sails and the strength of the hooves of the animals they used for transportation. The quest for knowledge brought scholars from across the Himalayas and across the seas to India and hordes of Indians travelled around the globe to assimilate Western thoughts and ideas. Knowledge could never be confined to geographical boundaries.

If globalization has merely accentuated a process that was already in place, it cannot have too many adverse consequences for education. But challenges there will be and education has to adapt itself to the new situation as it unfolds. Globalization has underlined the need for reform like wider utilization of Information Technology, giving productivity dimension to education and emphasis on its research and development activities.

Since education is one commodity, which gets enriched by every transaction, the more the interactions and the broader the reach, the better it is for education. The blessing of internationalization of education is that the wheel does not have to be invented again and again. The Internet has torn down boundaries and self-taught Ekalavyas will not be required to give the ultimate

Gurudakshina. Campuses have become irrelevant to a great extent except as meeting places of intellectuals and thinkers.

The challenge of higher education, then, is to make full use of the opportunities that globalization has provided. First and foremost, the marvels of technology must be fully and profitably deployed. In India, Internet connectivity for university students is still inadequate. But the massive increase in cellphones, which are becoming more and more versatile, may be the answer to India's connectivity crisis. Once full connectivity is accomplished, the students can be liberated from the classrooms and allowed to find and create knowledge. The universities will simply have to devise a means by which it can be established that the knowledge attained is genuine and accurate and that it is relevant to the needs of the countries concerned. Different students in the same class may diversify themselves and enrich different branches of knowledge.

One impact of globalization on education is the urgency to develop a skilled workforce at all levels to meet the demands of increasing business environment. Instead of its traditional role of providing education as a welfare measure, the state is required to facilitate privatization and deregulation in education, particularly as the quality of education provided by the state institutions has been rather poor. This is by no means undesirable, as privatization of education has helped to increase quantity as well as quality. Profiteering is a negative factor, but its evil is often offset by the timely and efficient utilization of human talent to develop competitiveness worldwide. Indians seeking employment and competing successfully is no recent phenomenon. Globalization has merely hastened the pace of migration and created better placements worldwide.

The likelihood of entry of foreign universities into India is an inevitable consequence of globalization. Top-class foreign universities are anticipated to add prestige to India's higher education. The expectation is that foreign universities will bring much-needed capacity and new ideas on higher education management, curriculum, teaching methods and research, together with investment. Though fear has been expressed that only commercial institutions will come to India and that Oxford and Cambridge will shy away, my guess is that top-class universities will come to India, not to make profit, but to profit from the vast intellectual resources of the country. The Foreign Universities Bill has adequate safeguards against throwing open our higher education to fortune seekers and unscrupulous business interests.

The advent of Public-Private Partnership (PPP) in education is also an offshoot of globalization. It is an innovative idea that can tap private resources for expanding the education sector. The Narayana Murthy Committee set up by the Planning Commission envisaged as much as 50% of the outlay for education to come from the private sector. Of course, the fear is that PPP will be used to compromise access, equity and quality. But a carefully controlled and coordinated infusion of private resources will benefit higher education. To try and keep private resources out of the campuses is to deny ourselves an opportunity to expand and strengthen higher education. The national commitment to provide good quality education will not be compromised if there is adequate legislation and just devolution of powers between the Centre and the States.

The anxiety about the impact of globalization on education arises out of its association with increasing social inequality within and between countries as well as instability and conflict. The dwindling importance of the State has also been a matter of concern.

Commoditizing of education and undue influence of private individuals and business houses are opposed by leftist ideologues. One of them argues that the entire education system must be informed by a certain perspective aimed at the creation of 'organic intellectuals' of the people who defend their freedom and their interest against the globalized order headed by imperialism.

The need of the hour is not to fight the onset of globalization, but to turn the challenges into opportunities. The best revenge against the forces that cannot be stopped is turning them to our advantage. Education is one area where it can be done effectively. Some of the measures suggested by experts to accomplish this are:

- Liberalization and deregulation of the education system;
- De-licensing higher education, conferring institutional autonomy and decentralizing syllabus design;
- Changing the role of Governments into facilitation and supervision through adequate regulatory measures;
- Upgrading teacher training, infrastructure and syllabus.

These are by no means exhaustive. Many more suggestions must emanate from conclaves like this so that we do not curse globalization, but turn it into our advantage. We must have the courage and confidence that a nation of India's stature, strength and size cannot be swept away by the forces of globalization. Like Mahatma Gandhi said, 'I do not want my house to be walled in on all sides and windows to be stuffed. I want the cultures of all lands to be blown about my house as freely as possible. But I refuse to be blown off my feet by any.'

ANNEX 8

Concluding Remarks at the Session on Knowledge and Education at Emerging Kerala

(14 September 2012)

I am delighted today, not just because I have the last word in this session on Education at Emerging Kerala 2012, but also because I have the company of another Ambassador on the dais. Normally, in academic fora in Kerala, I feel lonely as the only diplomat turned educationist here, but today I have the company of an Ambassador-at-large of Singapore. He spoke of many similarities between Singapore and Kerala. I have discovered one more: Singapore, like Kerala, sends unemployed Ambassadors to education!

I am also happy to see such a distinguished and packed audience at this session, including some from my own 'Cabinet,' the Member Secretary and other members of the Kerala State Higher Education Council.

I trust that I have been given the responsibility of making some concluding remarks after the rich debate today as I lead the Government 'Think Tank' on higher education. The Higher Education Council has the capacity, leisure and mandate to mull over new ideas and make policy recommendations to the Government. Note has been taken of the excellent suggestions made here by the speakers, who think, write and act on educational matters. I shall not summarize every speech that you have already heard, but outline what we have learnt from the erudite scholars. I am grateful to each one of them for sharing their thoughts with us.

The Honourable Minister and the Principal Secretary have laid out the Government's vision, its efforts, the systematic deficiencies of education today and the expectations they have of the outcome of Emerging Kerala. They have already indicated that higher education in Kerala is poised for exciting changes.

The speakers today were unanimous that education in Kerala has a good record and it has enabled its people to succeed nationally and internationally. At least in education, Kerala is not just emerging, it is emergent and wishes to re-emerge. Our graduates have competed with the graduates of the best universities in the world.

Many achievers in the USA and elsewhere have had their basic education right here and Kerala has contributed substantially to the reputation that the people of Indian origin, including Nobel Laureates, have acquired around the world. Even internationalization of education was not alien to Kerala. Many years ago, Maharaja Sree Chithira Thirunal of Travancore had invited Albert Einstein to be the Vice-Chancellor of our University. Needless to recall, the waves of Kerala migrants have contributed to the development of some developed States.

What is needed today, as the speakers have indicated, is to upgrade our education to equip our young people for the new opportunities and challenges of the 21st century. The India of 20 years from now will be far different from what it is today and we need to have a reformed system of education to meet its needs.

We need, what we may call in modern parlance, Higher Education 2.0. The contours of the new system have been identified and the Honourable Minister has announced that a new higher education policy will be unveiled soon. From what we have heard today, we need to address infrastructure needs, connectivity, research, faculty, autonomy and industry linkages, among others. I am glad to say that we have already initiated action in these very areas. We have recommended measures to the Government to remove the anomalies in the choice-based semester system and committees of experts are working on a new policy, a model university Act, a State accreditation and assessment Council, Institution–Industry linkages and a faculty training institution. Reform of higher education is very much a work in progress and today's discussions have given us a new impetus to proceed on these lines.

We appreciate the points made here that the industry should not merely look for graduates, but participate in planning and providing appropriate education and training to graduates, that faculty recruitment, training and deployment should receive adequate attention, that linguistic and communication skills of our graduates must improve, that curricula should be updated constantly and that education should be globalized. I am also fascinated by proposals for many innovative courses. For instance, a proposal has been made to establish a school for politicians, which will be very welcome.

We are heartened by the fact that substantial resources have been committed by the Central and State Governments for the reform of higher education. The best news I head at Emerging Kerala is that an IIT in Palakkad is becoming a reality. The Prime Minister himself indicated that the matter is under active consideration and the Chief Minister has announced that Kerala will get an IIT in the current Plan period. We greatly look forward to the fulfillment of Kerala's IIT dream. The indication of the Narayana Murthy Committee that the private sector would share half the cost of higher education in India is also great news.

Today's sectoral session on Knowledge and Education has shown that all of us are agreed on the need for the creation of Higher Education 2.0. The Government of Kerala has already embarked on this path and the views and suggestions made here will further embellish our efforts. I thank the participants for their contribution and assure them that their ideas would be fully considered.

ANNEX 9

Address to the Conference in Education

(Kerala Club, New Delhi, 16 March 2014)

I am grateful to the Kerala Club for inviting me to this timely seminar on higher education in Kerala. I have happy memories of my days in the Kerala Club in Connaught Place in the late 1960s when I met people like OV Vijayan, Kakkanadan, IKKM, MP Narayana Pillai and Sethu, who later became celebrated masters of the Delhi genre of Malayalam literature. Omchery was already a big name then and I am glad that he continues to lead the Kerala Club today. I extend my greetings and best wishes to the Kerala Club on the occasion of its Platinum Jubilee Celebrations.

I am glad that my turn to speak has come in the second half of the Seminar as it gave me an opportunity to reflect over the presentations of the earlier speakers. What occurred to me when I heard those statements was the saying about India that whatever you say about India, its opposite is also true. The same is the case with higher education in Kerala. Prof. NR Madhava Menon's contention that we need more universities in Kerala and Shri TKA Nair's apprehension that more institutions are not the answer are both valid. Whether we go by the cynical comments of Dr Jayakrishnan or the optimistic and poetic assessment of Prof. Meenakshi Gopinath, the higher education scene in Kerala has both good and bad points. It is true that many of our graduates are weak, compared to those from the better universities outside the State. But it is also true that three of our graduates occupied the three top positions in the Civil Services examination last year. Our accomplishments in higher education are not insignificant, but we need to strive more for excellence.

I take it that I have been included in this session on financing development of higher education since RUSA envisages that the Higher Education Councils will be entrusted with funding of higher education in the future, together with planning and monitoring responsibilities. But as it happens, funding of education is one area in which I have gained no experience in the last two years that I have been the Vice-Chairman of the Council. It is only a few days ago that the Government authorized us to open a joint account with the Government to receive RUSA funds and to begin setting up a Technical Support Group. Although the Chief Minister of Kerala is of the view that RUSA should be implemented strictly as envisaged by the MHRD, the process of empowering the Council to implement RUSA has been painfully slow and I have no hands-on experience to share as yet.

Although RUSA marks a paradigm shift in funding State educational institutions, I anticipate some problems in its implementation. Higher Education Councils have not been recognized as bodies capable of planning, funding and monitoring higher education, even in States like Kerala, which has had an active Council since 2007. At best, the Council is treated as a think tank or a sounding board and at worst as a sinecure for sectarian political nominees. The relevant departments of the Government and the Planning Board call the shots, and universities and colleges regard the Council as an unnecessary distraction, except as a source of scholarships and minor contributions for seminars and the erudite programme. The philosophy of RUSA that higher education should be entrusted to an academic body like the Council cannot be accomplished without political Will and relaxation of bureaucratic controls.

The problem is compounded by the fact that the States have to find 35% of the RUSA resources. The State machinery will be wary of the Council drawing up ambitious programmes as every rupee that is spent on RUSA, 35 paise should come from the State treasury. Moreover, the aided colleges, which make the bulk of the educational institutions in Kerala, will have to find 50% of the allocations made to them by RUSA. The present system of haphazard funding from multiple sources with little accountability will be preferable from the point of view of individual institutions. I have inaugurated many 'national' and 'international' seminars on esoteric subjects, held simply because a grant was received from one source or another. They become 'national' with an odd participant from Chennai and they become 'international' by the participation of a Sri Lankan scholar. Money is spent on ceremonies, flowers wrapped in plastic sheets and wooden or plastic souvenirs and even flex boards. The strict performance criteria of RUSA will be a disincentive to many institutions. A complete transformation of the mindset will be imperative. And mindsets, as you know, are not easily susceptible to change.

We can curse the darkness in many ways, but the efforts to light a candle to remove the darkness should also be noted. We have not removed the darkness as yet, but the Government of Kerala and the Kerala State Higher Education Council have not been idle. We started working from day one on a blueprint for designing what we called a 'Higher Education 2.0,' bearing in mind that fundamental changes are necessary in six areas we identified as crucial—infrastructure, use of technology, teachers' training, research, autonomy and internationalization. We set up groups of eminent experts on each of these areas and developed plans, which were submitted to the Government. These were not mere recommendations, but schemes ready for implementation. A Kerala State Accreditation and Assessment Council, a first of its kind in India, a Faculty Training Academy, a plan to link universities with industries, a new higher education policy with concrete suggestions for enhancing expansion, equity, excellence and employability, a plan for autonomous colleges and a scheme to improve the working of the administrative staff have been submitted. Initial funding was allocated in certain cases, but they are stuck somewhere in the labyrinth of political and bureaucratic decision-making. A report on reform of statutes of universities is unfortunately mired in a controversy on the qualifications of Vice-Chancellors.

Concretely, we have made advances in attracting foreign students to Kerala, developing cluster colleges, creating awareness of MOOCs and Flip Schools, TED talks and other tools for using technology, recommended honours courses in selected subjects and we have been running training programmes for young teachers and administrative staff. Seminars and conferences, including two international consultations on quality and transnational education have been held. Our monthly lectures focus on a wide variety of topics of current interest. Sage has just published the first issue of a high quality academic journal, *Education for the Future*. We are presently studying issues relating to Arabic studies, foreign travel of teachers and the possibility of setting up a university for Police Studies and Forensic Sciences. An area of concern we need to address urgently is the creeping elimination of English as the medium of instruction at the university level. A conference of foreign students in Kerala brought out the fact that much of the instruction is given in Malayalam, leaving these students in the lurch. In a situation where most of our young people have to live outside the state, the neglect of English will severely damage their prospects for employment. The Council is also looking at ways and means of incentivizing teachers, who put in their best.

The Higher Education Department runs its own imaginative Schemes for skills development, teachers' training, etc. in addition to their traditional role of nurturing higher education.

In other words, though we have not been able to submit our perspective plan because of the problems enumerated earlier, I dare say that we are more prepared to utilize RUSA funds than any other State in the country. But from a point of elation about the recognition of our work we received initially, we have entered a phase of frustration on account of delays and hurdles. We see a ray of hope in the small beginning we have made in implementing RUSA, but much more needs to be done to make the Higher Education Council an instrument of change.

Apart from RUSA, financing of higher education has to come from private sources. The self-financing colleges were instrumental in increasing the number of engineering colleges in Kerala. Some of these colleges can match the best institutions in India in terms of quality. A Commission led by Mr Narayana Murthy has established that at least half of the outlay in education should come from private sources. We have identified the ways and means to accomplish this, but the most effective way for higher education to grow is by having private universities. The policy of the Government, however, continues to be not to permit private universities in Kerala.

I apologize if my presentation sounded like a commercial for the Higher Education Council. I was merely trying to show that we are striving to change the higher education scene in Kerala. Change will be slow in coming in Kerala because of the cynicism that has crept into the Kerala psyche. Corruption, mediocrity, sectarianism, lethargy and lack of efficiency are not just tolerated, but also considered part of our system. Higher education sector is no exception to this general environment. But dream we must of good infrastructure, efficient use of technology, committed teachers, purposeful research, increased autonomy and international linkages, in short, world class education. We hope and expect that the Higher Education Council, which is presently a dream factory at best, will turn into a dynamo for true reform in higher education in Kerala.

ANNEX 10

Seminar on Autonomy at Sacred Heart College

Today, I not only inaugurated, but also stayed throughout the day at a Seminar on Autonomous Colleges at the Sacred Heart College. I am glad that the KSHEC co-sponsored the Seminar. It reassured me that the Autonomous Colleges will succeed in Kerala, despite hesitations, apprehensions and outright opposition to the idea.

Most aided colleges, chosen for autonomy, were represented and those who did not attend lost a good opportunity. The success of the Seminar was on account of two outstanding resource persons, Fr Dr Thomas Mathew, VC, Christ University, Bangalore, and Dr Nirmala Prasad, former Principal, MOP Vaishnav College, Chennai. The Principal and Manager of Sacred Heart College, the Provincial, Rajagiri Province, and the Dean and Administrator of the Rajagiri College not only struck an optimistic note but also underlined their commitment to making autonomy a success.

Expecting the usual cynical and pessimistic questions, I spoke passionately about the value of autonomy and stressed the courage and vision of the Government in my inaugural remarks. I also complimented the organizers for heeding my advice to avoid rituals, including flowers and souvenirs at academic seminars. During the interactive session, I discovered that I was preaching to the converted and the discussion was on other issues such as Faculty Training Academy and RUSA.

Fr Dr Thomas Mathew spoke eloquently of his experience of transforming an affiliated college into a university. He noted that the Kerala students had the least mobility and that our teachers were not able to transfer their brilliance to the students. Humility and strong Will, he said, should be the main qualities of a great teacher. He shared the excitement of liberation from the constraints of the affiliated colleges. Anyone who hears him will look forward to the academic freedom offered by autonomy.

Dr Nirmala Prasad was equally impressive in her presentation. She stressed the advantages of collaboration with industries, opened out by autonomy. She suggested that fears of extra work for teachers can be removed if technology is used for teaching as well as for holding examinations. The autonomous colleges will have the learning ambience of IITs and IIMs. Introduction of courses that combine academic programs with skills should be possible in autonomous colleges.

I know that several Seminars have been held on Autonomy, but this one was the most useful one that I have attended. We should have more such seminars, involving the designated colleges, including Government colleges.

I shall welcome comments and suggestions for making autonomy colleges a success in Kerala. There are already 441 autonomous colleges under 85 universities across 21 states. Why not in Kerala?

ANNEX 11

UNC-India Summit II at the University of North Carolina at Chapel Hill

(25 June 2014)

The campus air at Chapel Hill exhilarates me even though I have been on the road for more than 24 hours and I am not sure when the jet lag will hit me. It is indeed an honour to be invited as the Keynote Speaker at the UNC-India Education Summit II, 2014. I recall how the idea of Kerala-UNC collaboration at a seminar organized by the Wadhwani Chair of the CSIS a year ago, at which I made a presentation on the Kerala State Higher Education Council under the chairmanship of Ambassador Rick Inderfurth, himself an alumnus of the UNC at Chapel Hill.

Leslie Boney and Scott Simkins should be in the category of pioneers and explorers like David Livingstone and Christopher Columbus, as they came to the distant Thiruvananthapuram in Kerala State in their quest for new frontiers of educational cooperation. Today, we are reaping the harvest of their efforts by celebrating the growing cooperation between UNC and Kerala. I am here to reciprocate their visit and to see how far we can go on our path of collaboration. During the initial visit itself, they made a contribution to our thinking at the International Meet on Transnational Education (IMTE) as well as at the seminars in the Mahatma Gandhi University (MGU) in Kottayam and the

Cochin University of Science and Technology (CUSAT) at Kochi. Two more experts, Sanjiv Sarin and Jerono Rotich, have also been to MGU even within the first year of our cooperation. This Summit will give us an opportunity to assess the work of UNC not only in Kerala, but also in the rest of India. The pace at which UNC has begun to work in India is truly remarkable.

Leslie has asked me to place the educational reforms in Kerala and India in the context of the advent of the new Government under Prime Minister Narendra Modi. Neeraj Agrawal has already spoken of the prospects of the Narendra Modi Government from the point of view of a BJP insider. I share his view that there is much excitement about the change in Government and there is an air of new purposefulness in India. Many policies of the new Government are yet to be announced, but the indications so far are that there would be change, but also continuity, particularly in foreign policy. As for education, the concerned Minister, Smriti Irani, who was initially criticized for not having been to a university, has made a mark as a young, energetic and visionary person. A new educational policy is said to be on the anvil and all indications are that it is likely to be forward-looking, modern and technologically savvy. She has spoken of excellence in institutions in every State and the adoption of modern techniques of education, like the Massive Open Online Courses (MOOCs).

The Reports from Leslie and Scott have indicated the efforts we are making to build Higher Education 2.0, with six areas identified for special attention. The Central Government too seems to be introducing reforms, building on the good foundations laid in the past to meet the challenges and use the opportunities of the 21st century, particularly the demographic dividend India will have in the next few years. In my view, what is needed is not just a new education policy, but a new education system.

The new Government has inherited a substantially diminished relationship between India and the United States, compared to its heyday at the time of the India-US nuclear deal. President Barack Obama came to India in 2010 with the intention of building a defining relationship of the 21st century, expecting to benefit from the nuclear deal, purchase by India of military aircraft and the liberalization of the Indian economy. Those hopes have been belied for various reasons, most notably because of the policy paralysis in Delhi. The 'roller coaster ride' of India-US relations had reached a deep trough, with the Khobragade incident and the visa denial to Narendra Modi imposed in 2005. But as it has been made clear by recent events, the roller coaster has begun to move up again. Since the priorities of the Modi Government are domestic development and strengthening India's strategic space, the US will be a natural partner and the baggage of the past will be left aside. Prime Minister Modi is scheduled to visit the USA this September and no visa hassle is expected!

It must be remembered that even in the midst of the din and bustle of political controversies, quiet work in the various working groups has been taking place and education is one of the areas in which progress has been made. I have no doubt that this will continue and new areas of cooperation between the two countries will emerge. I hope that the modest success we have achieved in Kerala-UNC cooperation will be a contribution to the larger picture.

The Reports we have received today on the various ongoing programmes like UNC's Hindi-Urdu Language Consortium Program, its MOOC on the Asian economies, Social Work cooperation between UNC Wilmington and Bangalore University and others show how much UNC is involved in India already.

There was a time when India was hardly on the American radar—political, economic or educational. But today, India is very much in the consciousness of the US and the prospects are bright for multifaceted collaboration. From being 'estranged democracies,' the two countries have become 'engaged democracies.' The UNC-India Summit II has been a significant milestone in our journey together.

ANNEX 12

A *New Indian Express* Article on Education

(17 July 2014)

Smriti Irani, Minister for Human Resource Development, has spoken of a new education policy. The President indicated the contours of such a policy, stressing the need to use technology such as Massive Open Online Courses (MOOCs) and virtual classrooms and to create institutions of excellence in all States. The Rashtriya Ucchatar Shiksha Abhiyan (RUSA) seems to be alive and well. But what is needed is not just a new policy, but a new generation of higher education.

Poor infrastructure and technology, inadequately trained teachers, lack of autonomy for institutions, absence of a research culture and the failure to develop international linkages are the major reasons for the flaws in our higher education system. They are interlinked and need to be addressed through a holistic approach.

The RUSA document, which envisages a paradigm shift in higher education, addresses these and other issues. The thrust of its approach is to free the planning, funding and monitoring of education from bureaucratic controls. But most states seem to believe that education is too important to be left to the educationists. The change envisaged runs counter to the political and bureaucratic interests entrenched in the present system, but it must be pursued.

Simple living and high thinking are traditional attributes of students, but comfort and convenience are key to creativity, as we see in the best centres of learning. Brick and mortar are as important as brains and dedication for academic achievement. As we train our teachers in modern pedagogy and update their knowledge, online material such as MOOCs and TED talks need to be used liberally. The system of 'flip schools' should be adopted, making it possible for students to listen to lectures at home and do their homework in class with the help of teachers. Resistance to technology, combined with the lack of connectivity and even electricity, pushes us back to the blackboard age. The time is not too far when lectures in class will be outdated. Even the examinations of the future will take the form of 'gaming,' which tests the ability of students to tackle real situations. Innovation will come from hands-on experience, not from writing essays.

In the separation of universities from research institutions, the fundamental role of learning has been eroded. Patents of products and processes, and even Nobel Prizes, should emerge from the laboratories of universities. If Indian universities are not graded high, it is because research is not given priority. Exceptions like the Indian Institute of Science in Bangalore and Panjab University have been noted for their citations. Merging research institutions with universities and linking them to industries will ensure the pursuit of research with a purpose.

The affiliation system and bureaucratic control of funding have sapped the energies that autonomy gives. Things have come to such a pass that many students, teachers and even managements dread the idea of autonomy. When Kerala introduced autonomous colleges for the first time this year, there was widespread opposition. Academic freedom should lead to administrative and financial freedom, leaving the Government to fashion broader strategies and monitor their implementation.

Universities and autonomous colleges should determine what to teach, how to teach and how to evaluate the students. Globalization has brought international competition to our doors and we can exploit the demographic dividend only if we integrate our educational system with the revolutionary changes taking place in the rest of the world. Like political power, academic excellence is also moving from the west to the east. Our intellectual strength, the tradition of academic linkages with the world, our innovative skills and the cost advantages in India should attract international students, faculty and even great institutions. But we have isolated our education system by restraining contacts, making it difficult for faculty and students to go abroad. No serious effort is being made to attract foreign students to India. By offering courses that are unique to India and creating comfortable facilities, we should be able to attract foreign students to our shores. The success we have achieved in medical tourism should be duplicated in educational tourism.

Creating a new higher education system is by no means easy. Years of lethargy and the acceptance of mediocrity have created a mindset that is hard to change. Too many vested interests will resist change of any kind, not just stealthily, but also openly in the name of preserving the noble purpose of education against commercialization and commoditization. But unless India catches up with the education revolution around the world, it will not be able to realize its full intellectual potential. We need nothing less than Higher Education 2.0. We may not get on the list of world-class universities immediately, but we will be on our way there as the system begins to work.

ANNEX 13

Why Kerala is Making Drastic Changes in Higher Education Policies?

So far the Choice-Based Credit System (CBCS) has not been very well received in Kerala. To change matters, the Council has proposed adopting the UNESCO prescribed indirect grading system with a 7-point range. 'It is more dynamic, transparent and universally accepted,' says Sreenivasan.

Establishment of Faculty Academy

Identifying the dearth of quality teachers as one of the biggest challenges facing higher education in Kerala, the Council has proposed the creation of a faculty training academy. 'Access and equity have no meaning without quality education. Qualified, trained, passionate teachers are vital in any education system but hard to find in Kerala'.

KSHEC has received the State Government's nod for the creation of a residential training facility with the capacity to train hundreds of faculty annually. The Academy will offer three-months professional training modules for faculty being inducted and regular follow up programmes of varying durations for senior faculty. Courses will focus on communication skills, governance and leadership, ICT, pedagogic skills, personality development, professional ethics and values and research methodology.

Establishment of Assessment Council

To tide over the limitations of the National Assessment and Accreditation Council (NAAC), KSHEC has proposed creating a state-level assessment council. According to Sreenivasan, 'The UGC and the National Assessment and Accreditation Council have welcomed this move, which will help assess more colleges. It will also help implement the provisions of Rashtriya Uchchatar Shiksha Abhiyan in the state,' says Sreenivasan.

College Clustering

In tune with the UGC's proposal to establish college clusters, KSHEC envisages abolishing the university affiliation system in favour of College Cluster Multiple Campus Universities. The new concept entails a group of 10 to 30 autonomous colleges forming a College Cluster University. The university will be spread over multiple campuses and will only have its own centralized office to provide centralized examinations and academic monitoring. Constituent colleges will continue to be individually managed with their own respective fee structure. Clustering could be based on subject or location or financial status, etc. 'College clusters universities will improve the quality of higher education through sharing of resources, introduce healthy rivalries, and allow constituent colleges to receive the same UGC grants that are given to universities,' explains Sreenivasan.

As an experiment, KSHEC has organised clusters of 5 to 6 colleges operating in an area of 10sq km in Calicut, Kochi and Trivandrum. 'It is challenging to get private colleges' buy in for this concept. They see clusters as a burden, especially because of the presence of Government colleges. We are working on changing perspectives, to see college clusters as an opportunity for sharing and learning. So far, we are getting Government colleges in the clusters to create virtual classrooms so that students from other colleges can take benefit from certain lectures in the other colleges of that cluster. We have also given them small grants to improve their laboratory, sports, and other facilities,' shares Sreenivasan.

Catalyst for Change

'We act as evangelists for change,' says Sreenivasan about KSHEC. What are the expected outcomes of the measures that the Council has seen success for so far?

Sreenivasan expects autonomy to improve academic areas such as curriculum development, organization of courses of study, examination system reform, innovations in the pedagogy, induction of modern tools of technology to make learning student-centric, extending the academic calendar to maximize learning opportunities for students and designing of community outreach programmes to enrich the curriculum.

The new choice-based credit and semester system is predicted to facilitate intra- and inter-university credit transfers and ease postgraduate admissions besides making teachers more free to introduce academic innovations.

Faculty training aims at helping teachers apply and evolve new teaching technologies and aids, familiarizing them with trends in higher education, and helping them recognize students' differential capabilities and modify the method of teaching accordingly. 'We expect formal training to increase research and create a better learning environment resulting in more employable graduates and postgraduates,' says Sreenivasan.

As for the college clusters, Sreenivasan sees the Council's initiative as a small beginning for a better integrated higher education landscape.

Thanks to extensive groundwork, KSHEC is one of the Councils that is most prepared to implement RUSA. 'But we are yet to prepare a perspective plan for submission to the Centre because of the reluctance of the bureaucracy to accept the paradigm shift involved in RUSA, which entrusts planning, funding and monitoring to the Council,' says Sreenivasan. A change in mindset is badly needed for this Council to improve on these positive outcomes.

ANNEX 14

Education Must Be Up-to-Date

A Report by Meera Manu

(Published: 21 July 2014)

Taking a cue from world-class universities, efforts must be to create similar quality universities, says Sreenivasan. He adds that we have more or less achieved the primary purpose to make education accessible to everyone. 'We have to keep up with what is happening in the rest of the world, as education cannot be left behind. People in Kerala have to seek jobs not only in Kerala, but in other Indian states and abroad. So we have to catch up with the trends in education all across the globe,' he explains. He, in fact, says that 10 years is not enough for introducing reforms like changing syllabus, training programmes and making better use of technology.

Better Utilization of Technology

Sreenivasan points out the need to make use of available technological advancements. Utilization of MOOC, TED talks and Flip schools which are available free of cost are some of his suggestions. He opines that through MOOCs people can learn from the world's best teachers and professors and get a degree from any university they want. TED talks offer a plethora of subjects students can listen to.

In Flip schools, students can flip homework to the class and attend a class from home. At their own convenience, they can listen to the lectures recorded on mobile phones and use the time in classrooms to ask questions and get their doubts cleared, he says.

He feels that teachers now must learn more, and the present method of providing students what they already know will not suffice. They must use technology beyond emails and social networking. Above all, it is the mindsets that need to change, according to the former IFS officer.

KSHEC's Bit for Improvement

The objective of the Council is to advise the Government, universities and colleges on how to improve their quality and teaching methods. It does not leave the recommendations half way, but follows them up with the Government from time to time. It has identified six areas that require special attention—infrastructure, teacher training, use of technology, research, autonomy and internationalization. The Council makes action-oriented reports chaired by experts that are submitted to the Government, and puts them into practice after seeking approval.

Four Reports have already been approved by the Government. The report on Choice-Based Credit and Semester System is being implemented by the universities now. Focus now is on revamping the semester system. Based on the Report on Autonomous Colleges in Kerala, the Government has identified 13 colleges that can be conferred autonomous status.

The Report on Kerala State Faculty Academy on teacher training got approval and was sanctioned government funds. If the

Report on Kerala State Assessment and Accreditation Council is approved, Kerala will be the first State in India to have a State Accreditation Council other than the National Assessment and Accreditation Council, the nationally recognized accrediting agency funded by the Government.

ANNEX 15

All About a Change in Mindset

[TP Sreenivasan, Kerala State Higher Education Council Vice-Chairman, briefs G Mahadevan on the Council's achievements, aspirations, and limitations. Representatives of the Department of Higher Education and Kerala State Higher Education Council (KSHEC) participated in the discussions.]

Though the submission of our proposals was delayed for a year because the work on RUSA was not assigned to KSHEC on time, we worked from the day we were appointed the implementation agency of RUSA and submitted the proposals. Since then, we have been in correspondence with the Ministry of Human Resource Development (MHRD), which has been asking for various data, which were not easy to get. Our plans had to be modified several times because of the new conditions laid down by them.

The proposals are in the final stages and we expect to get an allocation before too long. Most allocations expected are for infrastructure development.

The Government decided that only the Government colleges and universities would be considered for RUSA funding in the first year. We recently requested aided colleges also to upload their plans, which will be considered for the second year.

The RUSA funding for the preparatory work has been received and it has been placed in a joint account of the department and KSHEC and is being utilized by mutual agreement.

What are the Reports generated by the HEC and submitted to the State Government and what is their current status? What, in particular, is the status of the Report on the Police University?

The reports on CBCSS and autonomy have been approved and are in the process of implementation.

The Kerala State Assessment and Accreditation Council (KSAAC) and the faculty academy have been approved and funds allocated, but the necessary structures, including their heads, are yet to be established.

The Cabinet is reported to have approved the Police University report.

The other Reports are under consideration of the Government.

During the tenure of the last LDF Government too many such Reports were submitted. Not a single one was implemented. Would your Reports meet with a similar fate?

As an advisory body, the most that the KSHEC can do is to prepare a blueprint. Our blueprint consisted of infrastructure, teachers training, and the use of technology, autonomy, research and internationalization.

As a think tank, the KSHEC has to generate a menu of ideas from which the Government can pick and choose. Since the Government has priorities and constraints, all our recommendations may not be implemented, as may have happened with the previous Council.

In the case of the present Council, the modifications to the CBCSS and the Autonomous Colleges Report have been implemented.

The KSAAC, the faculty academy, and the Police University have been accepted in principle. Our reports are action-oriented and can be used by the Government any time, depending on the needs and availability of funds.

Do you feel that the HEC should acquire or be given more teeth to bring about the kind of reforms suggested by various committees?

As long as the KSHEC remains an advisory body, it cannot act on its own. But the Council has responsibilities such as administration of the scholarship, holding of training programmes for teachers and administrative staff, publication of an international journal and commissioning of research studies. We have been performing these tasks.

One way to strengthen the Council is to entrust the administration of RUSA to it as envisaged by the MHRD. But the Council has been designated only as an implementing agency and the Department of Higher Education has retained all policy and administrative responsibilities.

This needs to be reviewed and the KSHEC should be empowered to deal with RUSA in consultation with the Government.

What do you reckon is the signature achievement of the KSHEC under your stewardship? What is the one thing that you would want to achieve before the completion of your term?

The signature achievement of the present Council is the creation of awareness to bring about major changes in education, leading to 'Higher Education 2.0' we proposed within six months of the formation of the Council.

A beginning has been made by the establishment of autonomous colleges, India semester programmes for foreign students, and teachers training programmes. We also expect that KSAAC and the faculty academy will be in place during the tenure of the present Council.

The one thing I would like to achieve is a change in the mindset, which resists all changes. I believe that higher education has changed globally more in the last 10 years than in the previous 100 years. Unless we catch up with these changes and reform the way we teach and learn, we will be unable to prepare our younger generation to make use of the opportunities and meet the challenges of the 21st century. This is very important looking at the demographic dividend we will have as the nation with the largest young workforce in the world.

ANNEX 16

Higher Education has Changed Globally More in the Last 10 Years than in the Previous 100 Years

[Remarks at the Indian Education Congress 2015, New Delhi, on 'Graduates of the 21st Century']

I should begin with a plea for anticipatory bail. I have been a professional diplomat, who strayed into higher education just four years ago. I have been trying to mix diplomacy with education!

My brief is very clear. I must speak to you about the requirements of successful graduates for the 21st century and outline the efforts made by Kerala to meet them in its institutions of higher learning.

Clearly, our higher education system is not geared for the challenges and opportunities of the 21st century. We need to catch up with the education revolution around the world, not only for our own needs, but also to avail of the demographic dividend on account of the largest group of young people in the world, India will have in the next few years.

Globalization and ITC have transformed expectations of graduates by the Governments, other employers and the society as a whole. The IT revolution, which came about without an owners' manual, needs to be deployed for the benefit of humanity. The paradigm shift in education requires the graduates of tomorrow to be versatile and engaging, with multidisciplinary knowledge to communicate, collaborate and solve problems with critical and innovative thinking. Ethical and moral development, cognitive and interpersonal skills are equally important. They should have lifelong learning by using ICT techniques such as MOOCs, blended learning and flipped learning. We need nothing short of a Higher Education 2.0 while the rest of the world is moving into Higher Education 3.0.

Kerala has many assets to cope with the transformation required. The 'Kerala Model' of development, which was the subject of a debate of the Titans between Jagdish Bhagwati and Amartya Sen, is a phenomenon in which, with modest economic growth, Kerala attained social development indicators to match the developed world. Education was a beneficiary, because of the imagination of the rulers of Travancore and the arrival of the missionaries. There was a Maharani, who declared that all expenses on education should be borne by the State. Kerala today has achieved access and equity in education, but its excellence is in question, as education has not moved with the times. The high literacy rate, linguistic skills, rich literature and individual successes in India and abroad raise expectations, but the education system needs to change and change fast.

We have a blueprint for change. Stress has been placed in improving the infrastructure, teachers training, use of technology in teaching, research, autonomy, internationalization and skills development. A whole menu of reforms is before the Government. Some changes have been made in the curriculum and teaching methods. Choice-based semester system has been introduced and autonomous colleges have been set up. Skill development has become a part of the education scene. But much remains to be done.

Kerala seems to lack the mindset to change and the money to invest in education. Some champions of change in all areas oppose changes in education. Absence of a prosperous private sector is also a handicap. Private Universities are still not permitted in the State. A State Assessment Council and a Faculty Academy have been on the anvil for three years. The huge gap between Kerala's capabilities in IT and the negligible use of technology in teaching needs to be filled. RUSA funding promised to usher in big changes, but the amount allocated is small and the areas indicated are not game-changing.

Kerala has the tradition and the potential to excel in education, but mindset and money are the factors that hold us back. We tend to leave things in God's hands. After all, it is his country and he should take care of it!

ANNEX 17

Transnational Education
Global Changes, Local Opportunities

[Prepared for the International Meet on Transnational Education, organized by the KSHEC, Thiruvananthapuram, Kerala, India, 3-5 January 2014—Muralee Thummarukudy PhD, Chief, Disaster Risk Reduction, United Nations Environment Programme, Geneva]

> *'In fifty years, if not much sooner, half of the roughly 4,500 colleges and universities now operating in the United States will have ceased to exist. The technology driving this change is already at work, and nothing can stop it. The future looks like this: Access to college-level education will be free for everyone; the residential college campus will become largely obsolete; tens of thousands of professors will lose their jobs; the bachelor's degree will become increasingly irrelevant; and ten years from now Harvard will enroll ten million students.'*
>
> —Nathan Harden: The End of the University As We Know It

CONTENTS

1.0 Introduction
1.1 Transnational Education—What is it?
1.2 TNE Definitions

1.3 Types of Transnational Education
- Distance Learning Programmes
- Certification Programmes
- Franchises
- International Branch Campuses
- Double Degrees and Twinning
- Online Courses and Tuition Support

2.0 Massive Open Online Courses (MOOCs)
2.1 What are MOOCs?
2.2 Tipping Point
- Accreditation
- Decoupling

2.3 Where is the Money in MOOC?
2.4 Winners and Losers
- The Million Dollar Professors
- A Million Teaching Shops
- Rebirth of Professional Bodies

3.0 TNE and India
3.1 Largest Unmet Demand of Higher Education in the World
3.2 English Literacy
3.3 High Internet Penetration
3.4 Familiarity with Accreditation Systems
4.0 TNE and Kerala
Bibliography

1.0 Introduction

Massive Open Online Courses (MOOCs) have become among the hottest topics in higher education in 2013. On one side are people like Nathan Harden, quoted on the title page of this document, who believes it will totally transform the landscape of higher education. Others are not so enthusiastic about its prospects of longevity, yet everybody is talking about it. MOOC is probably one of the most important developments in transnational education, with the potential to do significant good and bad to the higher education scene in the developing world. It is, therefore, important these issues are discussed, understood and planned for by the academic community all over the world. This background paper provides the reader with a macro view of this phenomenon and its potential impact on Kerala's (India's) education model.

1.1 Transnational Education—What is it?

Transnational Education (TNE) is an educational context where the student receiving the education is not in the same country as the institution offering the educational services. While TNE by itself is not new, the changes happening in scale of adaptation of TNE is already changing the landscape of higher education in the decades to come. A combination of technological, regulatory, academic and economic factors is behind this new-found enthusiasm for transnational education. This paper is an attempt to present the basic elements of TNE, its trends around the world, the role it will have in the Indian educational landscape and finally how Kerala can harness the potential of TNE.

1.2 TNE Definitions

Internationalization of education is not a new phenomenon. Students have been migrating from one region to another in search of good teachers for millennia and millions of students travel across the borders every year for higher studies in other countries. Transnational education is one of the subsets of internationalization of education but with the defining factor that it is not the student who is migrating towards the programme or university.

There are many definitions of transnational education and some of the definitions widely used and understood are given in Table 1.

Table 1: Definitions of Transnational Education

Name of Institution	Definition
Global Alliance for TNE (1997)	Transnational education denotes any teaching or learning activity in which the students are in a different country (the host country) to that in which the institution providing the education is based (the home country). This situation requires that the national boundaries be crossed by information about the education, and by staff and/or educational materials.
Council of Europe, Lisbon Recognition Convention (2002)	All types of higher education study programmes, or set of courses of study, or education services (including distance education) in which the learners are located in a country different from the one where the awarding institution is based.
UNESCO/OECD Guidelines for quality provision in cross border education (2005)	Cross-border higher education includes higher education that takes places in situations where the teachers, student, programme, institution/provider or course materials cross the national jurisdictional border.

The following are the key features of TNE that is evident in all of the definitions above and many more which have been proposed since:

1. The educational service is offered by an organization in a base country.
2. The students are also based in another country (or countries).
3. It is the educational service which is crossing the national boundary or becoming 'transnational.'

1.3 Types of Transnational Education

Distance Learning Programmes

The oldest form of transnational education is the 'distance learning programme' where an educational institution provides its academic content to learners outside its academic premises. This has been ongoing for more than a century and the earliest distance learning programmes were based on the course content being sent to the students for self-study. The students then take an examination conducted by the awarding institution to receive a qualification, be it a certificate or degree. While most of the recipients of the distance learning were from within the national boundary, there was no theoretical constraint to extending it beyond borders and TNE in its elementary form has been in existence since then.

Certification Programmes

In a variation of the distance learning programme, there were certifying agencies which conducted periodic examination in specific topics (e.g. English Language, computer networking skills, etc.) where students from any part of the world were eligible to take the exam.

The organization only ensured the integrity of the examination process and learners were free to undertake their study in whatever manner they deemed fit. Students were then awarded certificates on a pass or fail basis (as in the CCNA system) or on a continuous scale (like TOEFL). While these certifying agencies often produced study material and private entrepreneurs conducted coaching classes for the same, the certifying agency did not specify that the student follow either of the above as a precondition for appearing in the exams.

Franchises

A more rigid version of the certification programme was the franchisee system wherein the awarding institution prepares a standard syllabus (and often study materials) and provides franchisee status to a number of institutions around the world to conduct training on the same topic. While the tutoring, and often the exams, are conducted by the franchisees, the certificate is provided by the awarding institution. The awarding institution, therefore, is responsible for the quality control of the franchisees in the way they deliver the course content and conduct the examinations. The National Examination Board on Occupational Safety and Health (NEBOSH), a well-known certification system in safety, based in the UK, is an example of this system.

International Branch Campuses

International Branch Campus (IBCs) is a comparatively recent phenomenon whereby an academic institution in one country sets up a subsidiary institution in another country and offers similar academic programmes (mostly degrees). The IBCs may be full-fledged universities (like Australia's Curtin University's Miri Campus in Malaysia, or a lighter version like the New Caledonian College in Oman set up by the Caledonian University of UK). Table 2 shows the penetration of IBCs around the world as of May 2013.

Double Degrees and Twinning

Another version of TNE is where two academic institutions from two countries come together and offer joint programmes. Both teachers and students, sometimes both, cross international boundaries to offer and receive the training. At the end of the course, students either receive a degree from the institution in the home country, with the courses taken in the host country credited

Table 2: International Branch Campuses, Key Statistics, 2013

1	Total number of International Branch Campuses	188
2	Total number of host countries having IBCs	53
3	Country with maximum IBCs and number	UAE, 39
4	Single Biggest Cluster of IBCs	Dubai Academic City 23
5	Number of countries sending IBCs abroad (home countries)	24
6	Country with maximum export IBCs and number	United States, 88
7	Countries both importing and exporting IBCs	Australia, Belgium, Canada, China, France, Malaysia, Pakistan, Switzerland, UK

towards it, or receive degrees from both universities. In some cases, the two academic institutions award joint degrees to the students. This approach can be seen as a hybrid between conventional student mobility and TNE.

Online Courses and Tuition Support

The arrival of Internet changed the dynamics of TNE as the exporting of academic content around the world has become exceedingly simple. This is now progressing in multiple directions. First and foremost, certifying institutions are offering a large number of training courses online, conducting exams and awarding certifications. In another variation, many reputed academic institutions are putting their academic content online but not providing continued support or conducting examinations. In another type of transnational education, online tutors in developing countries are providing tutoring support to students elsewhere.

Table 3: Types of Transnational Education Models

	Distance Learning	Twinning/ Double Degrees	Franchises	Certification	IBCs	Online Learning
Student mobility needed	No	Some				
Times	No	No	No	No		
Tutor support given	No	Yes	Yes	No	Yes	No
Examination included	May be	Yes	Yes	Yes	Yes	May be
Certificates given	May be	Yes	Yes	Yes	Yes	May be
University credits included?	May be	Yes	May be	No	Yes	No
Cost	$$	$$$	$$	$$	$$$	Free to $

2.0 Massive Open Online Courses (MOOCs)

While all of the above has been in existence for more than a decade to a century, the current excitement in TNE comes from a few fundamental shifts in the online education scene which is threatening the very foundation of higher education. The following section details these developments.

2.1 What are MOOCs?

The term MOOC was coined in 2008 by Canadian researchers Dave Cormier of the University of Prince Edward Island in Canada and Senior Research Fellow Bryan Alexander of the National Institute for Technology (Canada) in Liberal Education in response to a course called Connectivism and Connective Knowledge (also known as CCK08). CCK08, which was led by George Siemens of Athabasca University (Canada) and Stephen Downes of the National Research Council (Canada), consisted of 25 tuition-paying students in Extended Education at the University of Manitoba, Canada, as well as over 2200 online students from the general public who paid nothing. MOOC was a logical outgrowth of the Open Educational Resources (OER) movement where many universities around the world put their teaching materials freely and openly in public domain for teaching, learning, educational, assessment and research purposes. MOOC moved on from this basic model to registering oneself as a student at a real or 'virtual' university which offered this course with a possibility to get graded.

While there is no single or authentic definition of MOOC, the following are the key features that can be identified as characteristics of MOOC.

1. The academic content of the course is made available free to the student.
2. The course content is delivered online, and all formats of course materials (text books, videos, interactive forms) can be used.
3. There no limit to the number of people who can take the course, hence it could be massive.
4. While it is not necessary for a student of MOOC to be graded, most MOOC platforms offer that as an optional extra.

In what has since become a legend in the higher education domain, a course in computer science, offered by Dr Sebastian Thrun from Stanford University was taken by 160,000 students from 92 countries. The experience so overwhelmed Professor Thrun that he quit his job in Stanford and set up his own online university, called UDACITY (pronounced YOU-DACITY, a play of words on You and Audacity) which is currently offering 25 courses with an academic enrolment of over 400,000. Since the Udacity experience, a number of new actors have come into the market and the most important ones are listed in Table 4 below.

Table 4: Providers of Massive Open Online Courses

Parameter	Udacity	Coursera	edX	Future Learn
Established in	2012	2012	2012	2012
For profit	Yes	Yes	No	
Funding	Sebastian Thrun and Venture Capita	Partner Universities and Venture Capital	30 Million Each for MIT and Harvard, 1 Million from Gates foundation + private partners	The Open University
Based in	United States	United States	United States	UK
Students from	Almost all countries	Almost all countries	Almost all countries	Almost all countries
Number of Universities offering courses	None	107	29	29
Subjects	Computer Science, Maths, Statistics and growing	Multidisciplinary, including medicine	Artificial Intelligence, Computer Science and growing	Science, Arts and growing
Medium of Instruction	English	12 Languages, 80% in English, followed by Chinese, French and Russian	English	English
Number of courses offered	25	540	91	29
Total number of students registered	400,000	5,427,051	900,00	N/A

MOOC platforms have also come on stream in Australia, Germany and China.

2.2 Tipping Point

While MOOC is already happening, the tipping point in their role in revolutionizing TNE will come when one or both of the following changes happen. These are accreditation of MOOC courses in the academic world and de-coupling between degrees and jobs in the labour market. Things are already happening in this direction but what is needed is widespread acceptance of these practices in the academic and real world.

Accreditation

One of the unresolved issues in the MOOC system is accreditation of the courses that are studied online. While conducting an exam at the end of the online course and awarding a degree have both become more or less standard practices of the MOOC system, universities around the world still have not accepted MOOC courses as equivalent to courses learnt in classrooms. However, a recent academic study conducted indicated that the learning outcome from an interactive online study and a course taken in a traditional formal are essentially the same when measured against pass rates and final scores (Bowen WG et al, Ithaka S+R, 2012). The same study also did a speculative cost simulation and found that adopting hybrid models for instruction in large introductory courses have the potential to significantly reduce instructor compensation in the long run. As the evidence base of such studies increase proving both academic effectiveness and cost competitiveness, there will be increased acceptance of MOOC in the academic world and in the labour market.

In most developed countries there are already systems for 'equivalencies' for certifications provided by professional bodies with qualifications acquired by attending academic institutions. Therefore, systems to evaluate and incorporate MOOC obtained credits into mainstream academic programmes exist and the fact that it has not happened is more related to the very cautious nature of the traditional academic community than any conceptual difficulties with MOOC. A parallel development to the accreditation challenge is already emerging. Online universities are already offering certification of the online courses they offer. Online universities are already getting into partnership with private enterprises to accept their certification for employment as well as promoting the jobs obtained by their students on their websites. A combination of these forces will break the resistance from the academic community to create a seamless credit transfer between the 'virtual world' and the 'real world.'

Decoupling

Higher education, for most people, is an effort to improve their employability and increase their chances of getting better jobs. Universities have traditionally taken on the task of screening the students for higher studies, putting them through a series of courses and awarding them with a degree to recognize their achievements. The labour market, in turn, uses the type of degree and the prestige of the academic institutions as a proxy for the employability of the student.

There is an increasing realization by employers around the world that the academic world is failing in its duty to produce 'employable' graduates. The academic rigidity of the university system teaches the students a range of courses and skills which does not correspond to the requirements of the real world. Also, while the requirements of the individual employer will vary, universities by their very nature can only have limited flexibility in their programmes which should prepare the student for a range of unknown potential, in jobs and employment. Consequently, on one hand the student has to learn a range of subjects he/she will never need in their future employment while the employer has to spend significant resources to retrain the new recruit to make them suitable for their organization. Employers can specify the range of skills they wish to have in their recruits and the students can acquire them from the provider who offers the most appropriate course. The employer may require a graduate from a specific university, or somebody who has done selected courses from prescribed universities or have been certified by an independent agency for their skill levels. The potential employees have the option to pick and choose their academic backpack based on the type of employment they are seeking. A combination of technical, computing, management and cultural skills will become the mandatory items in the backpack of any aspiring employee in future.

2.3 Where is the Money in MOOC?

One of the basic premises of MOOC is that the basic course is 'open,' meaning it is available free to the student. This, of course, is in line with the philosophy of the web where the basic product (be in search engines, social network sites or emails) are all given free to the consumer. The provider of such services then has to figure out how to recover their investments and make a profit.

In the traditional model of academics, it was the student who had to find the money to go to the prestigious university to learn a course. In the online world, it is now incumbent upon the university to develop and deliver the course online for free to the student. Naturally, the university needs to find the money to sustain its efforts. Where will the money come from?

There are many business models for a new university. The most obvious one is that while the universities may continue to deliver the basic content free online, they could charge the students for examinations and the certification. This model is already practiced by edX and Udacity. Because of the scale of the MOOC enrolment, in a course taken by 50,000 students (a very reasonable number for online courses), even if 10% of the students decide to get a certification paying USD 100, it can still bring in half a million US dollars in revenue. CEO of Udacity has reported that the overheads for a course with 160,000 students are covered by charging USD 1 per student. While the traditional academic model takes lot of money from very few students, the new universities can survive by taking a little money from a large number of students. (Reference: MOOCs and the disruptive innovation, the challenge to HE Business Models).

Coursera has identified 7 more possible sources of income in addition to certification which is the only current revenue stream. The additional possibilities identified are:

1. Secure assessments (students pay to have their examinations invigilated, which increase credibility of online course certification);
2. Employee recruitment (companies pay to have access to students' performance records);
3. Applicant screening (employers/universities pay for access to records to screen applicants);
4. Human tutoring or assignment-marking (for which students pay);
5. Selling the MOOC platform to enterprises to use their own training courses;
6. Sponsorships (3rd party sponsors of courses);
7. Tuition fee.

(*Reference:* Maturing of the MOOC)

However, the revenue stream opportunities do not stop there. Courses taught online could have a set of reference documents in it and publishers can then be provided limited time online access to those study materials and the revenue thus obtained can be shared with the course provider. One can also imagine a range of other academic and non-academic products and services sold to the student community through the platform bringing in revenue which is shared with the online course provider.

2.4 Winners and Losers

Like any new disruptive technology, there will be both winners and losers created by the higher education revolution. The biggest losers will be the hundreds of universities around the world which do not figure anywhere on the world university ranking indices. Once courses from the top-ranking universities are available, free of cost, to students anywhere in the world, there is very little incentive for any student anywhere to enrol themselves in an unknown local university. Internet has already redefined the famous rule from Jack Welch when he advised GE to be Number 1 or Number 2, or get out of the market in any sector. In the brave new world of Facebook, there is no room even for Number 2 and only Number 1 will prevail. The question we should ask is: 'will this theory be translated to academics as well?'Once learning goes massive, open and online, which brands of the existing universities will survive? The top 500, 100, 10 or an even lesser number? The answer seems obvious. When your option is to study a course free from any university in the world, why would you opt for the second best and why would an employer opt for a student who has chosen only the second best? So the arrival of MOOC will change the landscape of universities and in another 10 years one can imagine that there would be no more than a handful of recognizable university brands in the world. Let us, for the sake of understanding, call this the 'Facebook' university, as a reminder of how Facebook trounced competition even from the second best rival Orkut, supported by internet giant Google. A world in which only the top universities in engineering, medicine, law, music or commerce, will survive is very possible.

The Million Dollar Professors

In the current academic model every university offers similar courses and individual professors in all universities deliver the course to a group of 50 or 100 students at a time. For example, foundation courses like geometrical drawing or engineering mathematics is being taught in every engineering university/college in the world. In India alone there are more than 3000 engineering colleges and hundreds of thousands of students who take this course every year. Assuming even 100 students per class, there are at least 1000, probably many times that, to whom instructors are teaching geometrical drawing alone. It is very easily conceivable that an outstanding professor in any of the universities in India, or outside, can put a fascinating series of lectures online and that will become the basic teaching material all over the country. While all the 1,000 teachers in India now get more or less the same wages, it is also very conceivable that this professor with world-class pedagogical power will now be paid many times that by a company who arranges to sponsor his lecture and then charge a small fee from the hundreds of thousands of students who use his lectures.

A Million Teaching Shops

Once we take out the captive students from the current universities to global brands and follow the lectures from the 'super' professors, the question arises as to what will the thousands of universities and hundreds of thousands of colleges do in future.

There are two reasons why physical 'universities' and 'colleges' will not become redundant. Firstly, there are a set of subjects, such as engineering and medicine, which need practical learning. Local engineering and medical schools can provide such facilities even when the curriculum is set and student achievement is evaluated by a global university. Secondly, the local institutions can become examination centres where integrity of the evaluation process can be verified by supervised evaluations. Thirdly, a majority of the students who study MOOCs will need to get some degree of tutorial support. This is similar to the tuition centres that mushroom around colleges. Local colleges can easily rebrand themselves as tutorial support centres for global universities.

A more important aspect will come from the non-academic aspects of university education. Universities were not only meant to be places where students learned academic topics but also where they developed their social and leadership skills. While some degree of networking skills can be learned online, the cultural aspect of growing up would mean that young people come together where they can chat, make friends, date and have fun. The physical space of the colleges and universities can still fulfil those services.

The current university set-up will change in three ways in response to this transition. Firstly, there will be de-coupling from teaching and research. Traditionally, university professors conducted research, supervision and teaching concurrently and this will no more be needed as the high-end teaching gets taken over by the million-dollar professor and low-end tutoring by start-up lecturers. Research can be moved to research centres while teaching becomes tutoring. Secondly, the university space can become a centre for the microenterprise domain where individual tutors can deliver tutorial services. Such tutors need not be employed by the university as the 'university' provides nothing but a physical space where the tutor and student can meet. Thirdly, students will be looking for maximum flexibility and better infrastructure in obtaining their tutorial support and therefore some degree of consolidation of the 'teaching space' is inevitable. In the future, successful 'universities' in the third world will be spaces that offer the maximum cultural experience to the students.

Rebirth of the Professional Bodies

Widespread acceptance of MOOC at an administrative level could bring back a more prominent role for professional bodies, such as in the institution of engineers or bar councils. Historically, professions such as engineering, law and medicine only accepted a new candidate into their profession after the members have been put through an entry process which included technical training, practical apprenticeship and explicit commitment to professional ethics. However, mass production of engineers, doctors, lawyers and other professionals reduced the role of professional bodies to mere bystanders in professional education. A student could spend 4 years in an engineering college, obtain a degree in civil engineering and claim to be a civil engineer for life even though they have never undertaken any practical engineering at the entry to the profession of engineering or by the end of their careers. Professional bodies can once again set the entry criteria to professions which will include not only appropriate qualifications obtained through MOOC but also specify a duration of technical practice.

3.0 TNE and India

While the fancy lingo of TNE and MOOC may be new to India, the fundamental ideas behind it are not. India has already been practicing TNE even though there has not been any defined Government policy on the same. Due to the massive size of the country and the university system not being able to service all students aspiring to receive higher education, many of the elements of TNE has already been in applied in a national context too. Table 5 shows the type of examples which are similar to TNE which has been in practice in India in both transnational and trans-state fashions.

What India lacks, therefore, is not experience in practicing TNE but a policy framework which allows the country to take advantage of the new TNE revolution sweeping the world. India is well positioned to lead this revolution for a number of reasons:

Table 5: Examples Similar to TNE in India

TNE Element	Examples in India
Distance Learning	Indira Gandhi National Open University
Franchises	NIIT for computer education
Certification	Association of Chartered Accountants
Branch Campuses	AMU (Aligarh) Campus in Kerala MG University Campus in UAE
Online Learning	Amity University MBA Programme

3.1 Largest Unmet Demand for Higher Education in the World

India's population grows by about 20 million children per year. Assuming even 50% of these children study up to tertiary level, we are looking at 10 million students to be educated in colleges. While India has over 500 universities, a major portion of the Indian higher education happens within 30,000 colleges that are mostly affiliated to the State universities that have geographically defined catchment areas. The physical infrastructure, teaching quality and curriculum in these colleges leaves much to be desired. None of the State universities, to which these colleges are affiliated, is listed in any of the international university ranking systems. The employment market frequently complains that our graduates are not 'employable.' Even with all these constraints, obtaining admission toone of these colleges is still very competitive due to the number of students seeking higher education. So there are many reasons average Indian students will move en-mass to the new world of possibilities offered by the TNE.

- Availability of academic spaces as against severe competition in the geographically confined academic institutions.
- Possibility to study curriculum which are globally up-to-date.
- Receiving training from globally rated content providers and professors.
- Opportunity to acquire a combination of skills needed by the market as against the set menu of courses offered by the university.

3.2 English Literacy

India now has the largest population of students who are able to absorb learning in the English language, the language in which most of the TNE products are being generated and distributed. We could leverage on this factor to create the largest market for TNE which can then be leveraged.

3.3 High Internet Penetration

While physical infrastructure in India is still lagging behind, the digital infrastructure has caught up and the Internet, which is the key change agent in TNE, has high penetration among the student groups who form the primary target of TNE.

3.4 Familiarity with Accreditation Systems

India already has a system by which residency is no longer a criteria for completing qualifying competitions. The National Open School has done this for school education for generations and this model can be easily expanded to the university level. Setting a curriculum for various courses, establishing an examination system for courses studied online (even from outside the country) and a bundling arrangement for award of degrees are all possible with only marginal extension of the existing policies.

4.0 TNE and Kerala

The State of Kerala in India is a place which has very high potential for converting the TNE into a huge opportunity for enhancing academic standards, improving employability, increasing classroom diversity and massive economic opportunity.

Kerala is optimally placed to take advantage of the TNE for the following reasons:

1. High Aspiration and Mobility of the Population: The Kerala economy is based on a model whereby individuals obtain basic education in the state only to migrate to other parts of the country (or world) to take up employment sending remittances back home. There is thus a demand for globally current qualification and already a number of global certifications, like safety or computer networking, which even when not nationally recognized are widely sought after. So the Malayalee youth will take up the opportunity to obtain globally recognized qualifications via TNE opportunities even if they are not nationally recognized.

2. A very vibrant private sector which has invested billions of dollars of its own funds to establish higher educational institutions and have developed business models which bring them sufficient return on investments. Once familiarized with the TNE landscape they will easily find away to penetrate the market serving a social good in the process.
3. Well-established infrastructure (lecture halls, libraries, computer centres, housing facilities and other student activity centres), which, if efficiently used can teach hundreds of thousands of students per year, including offering of additional shifts if needed.
4. Higher education institutions see themselves as average 'teaching shops' with no pretention of research or high quality institutions. So for them to become 'franchisees' of a global brand is much less of an ego challenge than for the known national brands such as IITs or IIMs.
5. A good number of highly qualified academicians from Kerala who are currently working outside the state may be willing to repatriate if the financial incentives are adequate which could be achieved in an IBC context.
6. The State had a tradition of 'parallel colleges' which supplemented the traditional education market when the supply side was restricted officially. A MOOC-based training opportunity can instantly throw up hundreds of 'MOOC' tuition centres in the State where retired teachers, part-time teachers and young graduates, all, take on the role as MOOC tutors.
7. Moderate climate, stable political atmosphere and one of the lowest crime rates in the world making student life secure for students from other States and countries.

8. Low cost of training and living, especially compared to that of alternative locations (Malaysia, Singapore, Dubai or Qatar) which are currently leading educational hubs in Asia Pacific.
9. High connectivity with the rest of the world, with three international airports with more than 20 flights per day connecting to destinations in the Middle East, South Asia and South East Asia.

The challenge, therefore, is to increase awareness about the fundamentals of TNE among all actors, especially students, parents and private sector providers so that the social momentum for policy change is built up. There is also a need for an effort within the Government to create the correct policy regime and practical incentives to help the private sector and assure the students to move on to TNE and take advantage of the opportunities that have been created.

BIBLIOGRAPHY

British Council. *The Shape of Things to Come 2:The Evolution of Transnational Education*. Research Highlights. 2013.

Department for Business Innovation and Skills. *The Maturing of the MOOC*. Literature Review of Massive Open Online Courses and Other Forms of Online Distance Learning. 2013.

Observatory on Borderless Higher Education. *Horizon Scanning: What Will Higher Education Look Like in 2020?* 2013.

Observatory for Borderless Higher Education. *MOOCs and Disruptive Innovation: The Challenge to Higher Education Business Models*. 2012.

Open University. Innovation Report 2. *Innovating Pedagogy (2013): Exploring new forms of teaching, learning and assessment, to guide educators and policy makers*.

Muralee Thummarukudy

Muralee Thummarukudy is currently the Chief of Disaster Risk Reduction at United Nations Environment Programme.

Muralee holds a PhD in Environmental Engineering from Indian Institute of Technology, Kanpur. He is an alumnus of the International Leadership Academy (United Nations University) and a Beahrs' Fellow at the University of California, Berkeley.

Muralee has over 20 years of experience in Environment and Disaster Management around the world. Between 1995 and 2003, Muralee was Corporate Advisor to Shell-operated oil companies in the Middle East and South East Asia, dealing with oil industry related emergencies. He joined the UN Environment Programme in 2003 and has undertaken post-conflict and post-disaster environmental assessment projects around the world.

Higher education continues to be an area of interest for Muralee and he is on the advisory committee of the Center for Natural Resources and Development (Cologne University of Applied Sciences, Germany) and Center for International Academics (University of Kerala, India).

Muralee is a well-known blogger in Malayalam.

ANNEX 18

Thiruvananthapuram Declaration

[Adopted by the International Meet on Transnational Education, on 5 January 2014]

The Kerala State Higher Education Council

The Kerala State Higher Education Council (KSHEC) organized an International Meet on Transnational Education in Thiruvananthapuram, Kerala, between 3 and 5 January, 2014, which brought together over 100 academicians and academic policymakers from India, Afghanistan, France, Germany, Nepal, Netherlands, Sweden, Switzerland, United Kingdom, United States, Kenya and the United Nations.

This group, having debated various aspects relating to transnational education from a global, national and local point of view in 11 separate sessions over 3 days, have agreed to issue the following Declaration as the consolidated outcome of the International Meet.

The Thiruvananthapuram International Meet on Transnational Education:

- Acknowledging the potential role that transnational education can play in making quality higher education available to those desirous of improving their knowledge across the world without restrictions of national boundaries.

- Noting the explosive growth of the Massive Open Online Courses (MOOCs) and associated infrastructure, which are transforming the way educational content is delivered across boundaries.

- Recognizing the imperative to shape a strategy for higher education in Kerala in the light of international experience to catch up with the education revolution taking place around the Globe.

- Acknowledging the fact that the new trends in transnational education also has the potential to affect the capacity and legitimacy of national educational institutions and educational policy regimes.

- Noting the fact that currently there is no global framework which facilitates or governs transnational education and other related issues including quality control.

- Expressing concern that the national academic governance regime is currently inadequate to govern the complex nature of technology-enabled quality education.

- Taking into account that there are a number of global processes, such as the discussions on Sustainable Development Goals and the follow-up discussions on the education for sustainable development that are currently ongoing.

- Noting that a number of Indian universities have already taken the initiative to establish International Branch Campuses in other countries.

- Recalling that UNESCO has in 2005 issued Guidelines for Quality Provision in Cross Border Education.

- Acknowledging that developing countries, including India, have a number of structural inadequacies in areas such as language proficiency and last mile connectivity, which inhibit them from taking full advantage of online education.
- Taking into account that KSHEC has identified infrastructure, use of technology, teachers' training, research, autonomy and internationalization as areas for immediate attention in shaping a 'Higher Education 2.0' for the 21st century.
- Noting that the Government of Kerala has constituted an International Relations Group (IRG) to promote cooperation between the universities in Kerala and foreign universities.
- Acknowledging that KSHEC is currently engaged in framing an IT@Colleges Programme to improve connectivity in colleges.
- Noting with appreciation the initiative taken by KSHEC to call a timely International Meet on Transnational Education, which provided a platform for all participants to understand and deliberate on the opportunities and challenges posed by technology-enabled transnational education.
- Recognizing the Global Universities Partnership on Environment and Sustainability (GUPES) facilitated by the United Nations Environment Programme (UNEP), with focus on education, training and networking, including South-South collaboration.

Requests

1. The student community across the world to urgently take note of the rapidly changing scenario of technology-enabled higher education and new trends in transnational education and to supplement their learning opportunities regardless of their country, language, age and educational background.
2. The teaching community across the world to proactively consider the opportunities and challenges posed by technology-enabled transnational education and harness the potential to supplement and improve their own teaching approaches but also contribute to global learning.
3. The United Nations Educational, Scientific and Cultural Organization to organize a meeting of the Member States to discuss the formulation of a global policy regime, including an international convention on open education, which will harness the potential benefits of technologically enhanced transnational education for all Member States.
4. Academic policy makers in all countries, particularly the University Grants Commission in India, to urgently take note of the rapidly evolving scenarios of technology-enabled transnational education, such as MOOC, and formulate national policy regimes, including on quality control, which will ensure that the positive effects of this new trend are maximized.
5. Universities and other academic institutions around the world, including those in the developing world, to evaluate the new technologies of course delivery being promoted by transnational education with a view to harness the positive features of the new development to improve academic quality in their institution.

6. Government and other regulatory bodies to provide flexibility to academic institutions to engage in curriculum development, pedagogy and international collaboration.
7. Countries around the world to factor in the opportunities and challenges provided by transnational education in the discussing the follow-up to the Education for Sustainable Development decade (2014) and the Sustainable Development Goals (2015) which will most certainly have significant educational components.
8. Universities and Private Sector Organisations to work together to consider the changes happening in the academic regime, in particular, technology-enabled transnational education, could be harnessed to create a better trained workforce.
9. Government of India to establish a working group of academicians to review the implications of the new opportunities in transnational education and understand what the key constraints are for leveraging to improve access and quality of higher education in India.
10. Government of India to consider establishing a national online platform for delivering massive open online courses including in National Languages which will not only increase access of our students to best of our education but also train out universities to familiarize with such technologies.
11. Government of India to create policy regime to attract foreign students, including students from the Indian Diaspora, to study in Indian universities and academic institutions.
12. National academic administrators, such as UGC and AICTE, to establish a system of credit transfer, similar to

the European Credit Transfer System, which will enable increased mobility of students nationally.

13. Universities and engineering colleges, to consider the potential of MOOC and flipped classrooms to supplement the current training approaches especially in topics where there is severe shortage of qualified faculty.
14. Private sector in India to collectively consider how opportunities of transnational education can be leveraged to provide continuous learning opportunities for their employees as is already practiced by many multinational corporations (MNCs).
15. Government of Kerala to establish a committee, including representatives from academics, private sector and the Malayalee Diaspora, to review the opportunities created by the recent changes introduced by the Government of India on allowing International Branch Campuses.
16. Director of Technical Education (Kerala) to conduct a study of the high failure rate of students in engineering programme to see if it could be partly addressed by the opportunities offered by technologically enhanced learning.
17. Kerala State Higher Education Council to conduct a series of road-shows on Transnational Education across Kerala to increase awareness about its opportunities among academic decision makers, teachers, students and private sector across in Kerala.
18. Kerala State Higher Education Council, along with Malayalam and Sanskrit Universities to review what is the potential for developing and delivering Niche Open Online Courses (NOOCs) on global platforms such as edX and Coursera in niche areas.

19. Kerala State Higher Education Council to establish an online community of practitioners, including those who attended the Thiruvananthapuram International Meet of Transnational Education so that the dialogue and information exchange could continue.
20. The private sector educational providers in Kerala to leverage Kerala's reputation as a friendly and economical global tourist destination to market their capacity to deliver quality higher education at affordable costs across the developing world in order to attract more international students to come to Kerala and increase diversity in classrooms.
21. Kerala State Higher Education Council to establish a Committee of Experts to study the possibility of recommending to the Government of Kerala to permit private universities in Kerala to enhance direct investment in the higher education sector.
22. Requests the education stakeholders to make full use of the Academic Journal of the Kerala State Higher Education Council 'Higher Education for the Future' which was released at the meet.
23. Requests the Government of Kerala to recognize and enforce governmental regulations for ensuring social and economic justice and making quality TNE accessible to the marginalized.
24. Requests that the implementation of MOOC should be done by considering the students with special needs.
25. Requests a feasible financial model to generate additional resources for further growth of off-campus institutions and to take up measures to improve the quality of the curriculum.

26. The United Nations Environment Programme to promote South-South collaboration through the Global Universities Partnership on Environment and Sustainability (GUPES), and solicit the active participation of universities, including those from Kerala, on transnational education and training on sustainable developments issues.
27. The United Nations Environment Programme to share the Thiruvanathapuram Declaration on Transnational Education at the World Conference on Education for Sustainable Development commemorating the end of the UN Decade of Education for Sustainable Development 2005-14, which will be convened in Nagoya, Japan, during 10-12 November 2014.

The participants of the International Meet on Transnational Education further resolve:

- To continue the discussions individually in coming days in their respective countries, academic forums and educational institutions they represent, to harness the potential of transnational education.
- To explore opportunities to collectively come together in 2015 at another venue to continue the discussion, including increased participation from the providers of transnational education.
- To promote, in their respective countries and sphere of influence, the relevant conclusions from the Thiruvananthapuram Declaration on Transnational Education.

The Kerala State Higher Education Council, the hosts of the International Meet on Transnational Education to widely publicize the Thiruvananthapuram Declaration on

Transnational Education so that students, teachers, academic policy makers and other stakeholders of higher education can use it as a basic document to advocate and promote transnational education.

- The participants of the International Meet on Transnational Education express appreciation to the Kerala State Higher Education Council for the excellent arrangements and warm hospitality.

Issued in Thiruvananthapuram, on 5 January 2014.

ANNEX 19

Global Education Meet, 2016

Theme Paper

Preface

I am pleased to transmit to the participants of the Global Education Summit, 2016 a Theme Paper, prepared by a Committee of eminent academics, chaired by Dr Murali Sivaramakrishnan, Professor, Department of English of the Pondicherry University. A list of the members of the Committee is annexed. I place on record my sincere appreciation for the work of the Committee, in which I participated throughout.

The Theme Paper is the outcome of extensive discussions and exchanges among the members of the Committee, bearing in mind the major objectives of the Meet, such as enhancement of international cooperation and fashioning of an Academic City and International Higher Academic Zones. The paper seeks to provide to the Meet an outline of the relevant issues, their background and the possible direction that the discussion might take. But it is neither comprehensive nor restrictive and the Meet is free to add to or subtract from it. The idea is to facilitate a vibrant and productive discussion.

We expect to encapsulate the discussions at the Meet in a 'Kovalam Declaration on Making Kerala a Hub for International Education.' The recommendations on policy and practice will be submitted to the Government of Kerala, the Kerala State Higher Education Council, the Ministry of Human Resource Development, the University Grants Commission and other stakeholders.

I hope that the participants will have an enjoyable stay in Kerala and fruitful discussions at the Meet.

Ambassador (Rtd) TP Sreenivasan, Vice-Chairman,
Kerala State Higher Education Council
17 January 2016

* * *

Global Education Meet, 2016

Theme Paper

Educational systems need necessarily reflect the pace and quality of transformation taking place in other walks of life so as to evolve in tandem with the times. The State of Kerala, having pioneered and initiated several models of development over the years, has naturally come to recognize its new role in reforming and adopting nascent models in the field of higher education. Radical changes have to be effected in the modes and methods of teaching, learning and evaluation in order to accommodate the compelling requirements of an emergent world, and reforms in higher education are urgently required in the following areas:

- Infrastructure
- Training of teachers

- Technology-based Teaching and Learning
- Autonomy
- Research
- Skills Development
- Internationalization

Higher Education in Kerala

Education at all levels has been in high demand in Kerala even from early days, and the State has always been committed to providing fair and equal opportunity for everyone. It is noteworthy that a significant portion of the Government's revenue is set apart for education. However, development and modernization of higher education in Kerala has not, till date, attained the desired objectives in full measure. This is certainly an area that calls for immediate attention and reform.

Even with its 100% literacy rate and higher gross enrolment ratio (GER), Kerala is still struggling to offer its young people diversified range of courses that the global and national economy of the day requires. In spite of their high demand in the State, future-oriented courses with high employment opportunities are still few, what with most colleges choosing to offer only conventional courses in a conventional manner. This is evident too from the fact that a large number of students prefer to go to private universities and private colleges in the neighbouring States of Karnataka and Tamil Nadu, even while a sizable number of seats, including those in technical and paramedical courses, lie vacant in private and government colleges in Kerala. This paradoxical situation arises because over-indulgent parents are even ready to bear any additional cost and dare other risk factors while admitting their wards in some far-off, little-known colleges (many of which do not have even the required accreditation, qualified faculty or proper facilities). Consequently, thousands of students move out of the State annually in search of innovative higher educational opportunities elsewhere.

Besides this, a large number of students from the State flock to universities abroad, in the USA, UK, Australia, China, Russia and other countries; most of them register for the new and emerging courses of study, especially in science and technology, medicine, commerce and management. This massive migration of students to other States and abroad definitely causes a huge drain on the State capital. What surfaces is the fact that the existing higher education system fails to satisfy the needs of students. This situation demands urgent attention and remedy.

Transnational Higher Education: Education and Global Trade

With the increasing importance of the service sector in the world economy, the member countries of World Trade Organization (WTO) in 1996 signed a General Agreement on Trade in Services (GATS) which covered services of international trade at par with merchandise trade. This agreement in general covers all the services (presently 19) including education services. Although the linking of an ethical process like education to global market and trade may be considered inappropriate, the issue highlighted by this agreement is worth exploring. In its recommendations, the WTO Committee observes:

> There is a need to encourage private participation with adequate social control through appropriate incentives in higher education with a view to enhancing access by increasing capacity, supplementing government funding and making higher education

> closer to the job market. This would also facilitate healthy stimulation through competition. For this purpose, an enabling environment and a coherent policy framework ensuring transparency, accountability and effective quality assurance mechanism should be worked out.

Education may not be compatible with trade; neither might it be appropriate to equate the process with competition and market values, but in the light of a changing world, where job markets proffer substantial profit and consequent creature comforts accruing through the same, it would certainly be in the scheme of things that a fast internationalizing scenario caters to the student community in an appropriate and befitting mode and method, enhancing their access by combining private participation alongside. It might be apt at this point to draw attention to the fact that there is now in India's foreign economic policy a greater emphasis on enhancing earnings from services, particularly in the broadening areas of tourism, entertainment media, healthcare and education, and also in harnessing the private sector in the pursuit of the country's economic interests abroad.

While most states have offered significant amount of autonomy to their educational institutions to enter into coalition with whomsoever they may deem fit at their institutional level (although several issues surface around recognition at the national level), many higher education institutions in India have expressed interest in collaborating with specific countries, including the UK, USA, Canada and Australia. So then, while international collaboration in higher education is still in its nascent stages in India with apparently no clear international strategy in place yet, the increasing focus on quality, research and student or faculty exchange, supplemented with government initiatives and state encouragement does offer significant opportunities for collaborative efforts.

A Brief Look at the Current Scenario

It might not be out of place to point out that the people of Kerala are second to none when it comes to intelligence, enterprise and hard work. There is little cause to doubt the intellectual capability and commitment of the student community in the State. That the society of Kerala accords great importance to higher education is also a well-known fact. The literacy movement found a significant space in the State. In primary and secondary education, the state marched quickly ahead of many regions, not only in India, but in most parts of the world. But in the arena of higher education, particularly with regard to its quality, global standards, innovation, responsiveness, academic brilliance, creation of new knowledge, research orientation, research publications in Journals of international repute, interface with industry, interface with general society and the like, there is certainly a hold-up. In terms of global rankings, none of the State's institutions figure anywhere in the list of the top 200.

While it is a generally accepted fact that there is no dearth in the enthusiasm and enterprise of the student force in the State, it is equally true that the current educational machinery and university systems fail to cater to their needs, as stated. Many educationists point out that traditional approaches and applications to placate this demand may neither be sufficient nor suitable at this juncture. What is interesting is that the country has perceived a dramatic shift towards private provisions across the entire education spectrum, including higher education, and the private sector is already playing a significant role in the development of education in India—and its influence and presence will, over the years, increase substantially. The private sector, which currently accounts for a significant percentage of all enrolment, continues to grow rapidly, providing space for most of the professional courses, particularly in engineering and management. Many more providers are waiting for legislation, which would allow them to enter the global market. The private sector, no doubt, is expected to play a significant role in the future expansion of higher education in India, and it would be worthwhile at this stage to explore the possibilities of harnessing this force to transform the current educational scenario.

However, there are increasing signs of a growing caution on the part of educators and intellectuals toward the State resorting to private enterprise—a reserve that may be informed in part by a growing body of research cautioning that 'expanding for the sake of expansion' carries a high risk of failure. It also underscores a growing awareness of the innumerable challenges associated with international campuses, which have opened out to investors and private interests, which need to be drastically addressed. Notable among these challenges are the issues of financial viability and quality assurance. Some other factors include easier facilitation of credit transfer systems, movement between the higher education and vocational-skill streams, and of course equipping of teachers with specific skills. Initiatives have already been taken to address these issues.

International Collaboration

Recognizing the compelling pressures of globalization and consequent transformation of the educational system in a befitting international manner, it is worth drawing attention to some modes and methods of such international collaboration. A list of possible collaborative programmes could include the following:

1. **International Dual-Degree Programme:** Any aspiring student can opt for pursuing a degree course in tandem

with an international partner university. This would provide an opportunity for a student to obtain additional degree or diploma along with a similar degree from the parent university.

2. **International Integrated Dual-Degree Programme:** This programme offers options to the student for pursuing a degree or part of the degree in the parent university and the remaining portion of the degree and the postgraduate programme in an international partner university. This would be an opportunity for a student to obtain additional undergraduate and postgraduate degrees along with the degree of the parent university and vice-versa.
3. **International Twining Programme:** A student can opt for studying a part of the course or semester of the degree in an international partner university to complete the course of study.
4. **Study Abroad Programme:** Under this programme, a student can pursue a certain period semester of his/her course, especially for the projects/ internships etc. in an international partner university.
5. **International Student Exchange Programme:** Through this programme students can pursue the required number of credits of the course of their choice, especially for specific or regional speciality subjects/ specialization etc. in an international partner university and the credits accrued can be used for completing the course.
6. **Summer/Winter Schools:** Under this programme, students get the exposure of learning from eminent professors from the internationally reputed partner university.

7. **Joint Research Collaboration:** Joint research activities with international partner universities proffer unlimited possibilities. Quite a lot of research funds are also available locally as well as from abroad through research funding agencies for such programmes and the like.
8. **Faculty Exchange/Visiting Scholars/Sabbatical Professorships:** Faculty exchange is usually the most effective way toward developing a diverse set of knowledge reserves in a challenging intellectual environment. This is possible either by sending our faculty to international partner university or bringing their faculty to our institutions. Fulbright Scholarships, sabbatical leave for faculty and the like are some such programmes that aid the student and faculty alike.
9. **ICT-Enabled Joint Teaching:** With ICT support, different models of integrated teaching can be developed for the benefit of both students and teachers of different universities worldwide.
10. **Joint Conferences/Seminars/Workshops/Training Programmes:** Effective knowledge creation and dissimilation, capacity building and exchange of ideas could be made possible through jointly organized conferences/seminars/workshops/training programmes and such similar activities with international academic partnerships.

The prospect of acquiring a degree from a foreign university would certainly motivate possible academic promoters in India, because it would naturally ensure promising future international placements, scholarship assistance and the like for enterprising students. Further, a significant reduction in the fee structure in comparison with similar institutions abroad, plus the delectable opportunities for acquiring international experience by spending a semester in the partnering institution, and an overall professional development would be encouraging factors. The dramatic expansion in numbers of students seeking higher education abroad these days, and a significant rise in the number of partnerships with foreign institutions, are all, as we know, due to political and societal changes in the domestic and national front. However, these current internationalization activities proffer their benefits only to a small percentage of the relevant age group, which could lead toward eventual social disparity; therefore, government intervention is certainly called for.

Now, in order to promote cultural understanding through education, the Government of India has been offering many fellowships to international scholars specializing in Indian studies in the fields of humanities, culture and social sciences through the Indian Council for Cultural Relations (ICCR). Kerala is also one of the destinations for these scholars. The ICCR has established 108 Chairs of Indian Studies in various foreign universities. However, the remarkable growth of transnational education providers in the Indian higher education scene has been a more recent phenomenon.

The emergence of the new global environment has dramatically reshaped the country's higher education system which has created tremendous opportunities for internationalization, especially transnational or cross-border education. The dramatic expansion in the number of students going abroad and a significant rise in the number of partnerships with foreign institutions is an example of this growth as we have noted. Apart from this, the inward mobility of international students to Indian institutions has also been increasing in recent years with the majority of the foreign students coming to India from Asian and African countries and even a trickle from developed nations.

Agenda of GEM 2016

GEM is visualized as a platform to debate and discuss the modalities of this imminent transformation in our higher education system. Discussions could centre around the following points:

- Modalities of partnerships with international universities—MOU, Twinning and such similar activities.
- Setting up of international academic centres in line with National and State Educational Policies.
- Establishing International Higher Academic Zones with global standards and state-of-the-art facilities in the metropolitan cities in the State.
- Creating an Academic City with adequate built-up space and state-of-the-art facilities to be provided by the State Government for furthering higher education.

International Higher Academic Zones

One of the means to accomplishing the essential goal of internationalization is through the creation of specific International Higher Academic Zones (IHAZs) with suitable and sizable private participation. This could be achieved through extending invitations to institutions which have already established meritorious associations with renowned international universities, proffering quality education to students of all nations in state-of-the-art campuses.

IHAZs, in a Public-Private-Partnership (PPP) mode, are generally expected to proffer futuristic, technology-assisted and world-class higher education catering to the educational demands of the next generation of Indian and foreign students. IHAZs are also expected to adopt innovative academic approaches and globally accepted benchmarks in order to make them the sought-after destinations for higher education.

In the Budget Speech for 2015-16, the Government of Kerala has already announced a scheme to take steps to project Kerala as a preferred international destination for education in India. IHAZs are proposed to be opened in various parts of the State with sizable private-sector participation.

The IHAZs will be created for which the State Government is to offer facilities and incentives at par with those offered in the Special Export Processing Zones (SEPZs) set up in the State. This will include water supply, power, roads, an exemption from registration fees and other taxes, which would be subject to the condition that 25% of the total fee collected in the Zone will be set apart for a Scholarship Fund for students in the public educational institutions who qualify for admission to the institutions in the Academic Zones. It is also desired that each IHAZ will have an area of not less than 20 acres and will host academic courses from reputed international universities.

Academic City

The Government intends to create an Academic City in one of the metropolitan cities with a vast area and state-of-the-art facilities where educational institutions could establish centres of excellence with national and international collaboration in the self-financing mode.

Objectives of the IHAZs and Academic City

The International Higher Academic Zones, or the Academic City shall have facilities for study, training and research in multiple disciplines. These shall also promote employable and career-oriented, high-quality academic programmes and shall strive:

- to impart quality education offering the scope for inter-disciplinary and intra-disciplinary study on par with the standards and parameters of education offered on international level through various graduate, postgraduate, research, diploma and certificate programmes;
- to contribute to the progression of higher learning with its various disciplines and specializations while offering courses that are of the finest quality;
- to invent and execute educational strategies which are pertinent to the present needs and long-term requirements of the society and receptive to the predictable alterations and developments of the future scenario;
- to establish modern and innovative research and development centers to facilitate the utilization and widespread awareness of contemporary technology for the overall benefit of the society and multi-sector development of the State;
- to collaborate and establish collaborations with reputed universities, research institutions and laboratories, libraries, and other research and development centers worldwide for promoting joint academic research and extension activities for mutual benefit and interest;
- to conduct joint and collaborative research programmes and activities with approved Government-aided research institutions like DST, CSIR, ICAR, DBT and DIT;

- to provide best available sports, cultural, literary and academic support programmes and activities for the aspiring students;
- to create a full-fledged developed community in and around educational and research environment;
- to continue to maintain the existing courses of the colleges while introducing new and innovative courses, research and programmes in various academic disciplines and inter-disciplinary areas in a phased manner as per needs, aspirations and requirements of the State.

Revenue Projections

Sources of income other than the sponsoring agency's contributions, donations and other sponsorships would be limited to the fee generated for the purposes of tuition, admission, registration, hostel, co-curricular activities, consultancy and service charges from the students. External funding and income from R&D would also be other sources of revenue. A Sustainable Revenue Model for the operation of IHAZs and Academic City would be developed based on consultative discussions with all those involved.

Financial Viability of IHAZs and Academic City

Education, it is recognized, is not a commercial activity and hence the IHAZs/Academic City should not operate purely on a commercial basis. However, taking into consideration the costs involved in such huge establishments and the still larger recurring costs likely to crop up over the first 10 years of inception, it could happen that the IHAZs/Academic City may soon find it difficult to attract sufficient number of students to completely offset those recurring expenses and interests on capital. There is also the implied fact that only through the maintenance of fine quality can educational institutions attract and retain large number of students, which could also help to maintain its fiscal needs, but it follows, necessarily too, that higher quality can be attained only by accruing massive investments.

Now, for the potential investor in IHAZs/Academic City, the major motivating factor would be the visible commitment to the cause of quality in higher education and the aura of prestige that the investing institution will acquire in the process. The investor would need to bestow money constantly and perhaps reap very little profit out of the process, because the income generated would be ploughed back in. The dividend to the sponsor might accumulate principally as prestige, reputation and societal influence. It will also go a long way in fulfilling their corporate or institutional social responsibility (CSR). It is a point worth highlighting that several such agencies have already shown interest and submitted formal proposals through the required expression of interest called for.

The Government of India has initiated several measures to tackle the challenges to the system by setting up various measures to improve the employability of Indian graduates and to position India prominently on the global higher education landscape through initiatives in skills-development, digitization and research. It is quite encouraging that while preparing a new policy for education nearing completion this year, several new flagship initiatives, specifically related to potential international collaboration, have recently been launched—renowned international universities have been invited to offer postgraduate courses in the disciplines of social sciences, basic sciences, engineering and energy, and sustainable development.

Advantages of IHAZs/Academic City

IHAZs/Academic City can attempt to create a higher education system that ranks among the world's leading education systems and which will enable Kerala to compete in the global academic standards and economy. Such zones/cities:

- will usher in considerable amount of private funds for the advancement of higher education, reducing the state's burden;
- will have to rely on excellence and quality to ensure survival and, therefore, will be continually responsive to emerging trends;
- can instill an entrepreneurial mindset in higher education system and create a system that produces qualified personnel with a drive to create jobs, rather than mere job seekers searching for a livelihood;
- will address a system that is at present less focused, by placing emphasis on integrating the established traditional academic pathways and the much-needed technological skills, career as well as professional training;
- can focus on outcomes over inputs and to actively pursue technologies and innovations that address students' needs and enable greater personalization of the learning experience;
- will enable transition from the current, highly centralized governance system to a new model, based on academic autonomy within the regulatory framework which prevents wanton abuse and wastage;
- will promote the flow of students from other parts of the world—particularly from West Asia, South Asia and East Africa—by diversifying and raising the quality of the programmes offered.

Academic City Authority

An Academic City Authority (ACA) is proposed to be constituted with a mandate to regulate and monitor the functioning of both the IHAZs and Academic City, with a focus on quality higher education. The proposed ACA will comprise representatives of the Department of Higher Education, KSHEC, universities, national institutes, MHRD, MEA and academicians of national and international eminence. The ACA's role would also include:

- the issue of regulations/guidelines for the setting up and the functioning of the IHAZs;
- the granting of permission to promoters for establishing IHAZs;
- overseeing the setting up of IHAZs and their operations as per the approved regulations;
- ensuring total quality of systems and processes in the IHAZs;
- renewing permissions to IHAZs based on quality and academic audit reports.

It shall be mandatory for the IHAZs/Academic City to comply with the regulations made by the UGC, and the ACA shall have powers to monitor the maintenance of standards of degrees and other programmes offered by the institutions, and for forestalling possible commercialization of education. It is mandatory and necessary that the IHAZs and Academic City are well regulated and effectively monitored by the ACA.

Conclusion

The major thrust areas of the 12th Plan regarding higher education in India highlight inclusion and excellence. It has also become necessary to increase the GER of students in order to accelerate the development prospects on a larger scale. Sole dependency on the current state-run educational institutions may not yield suitable results. Further, the state is seriously handicapped when it comes to the matter of huge financial resources required as investment to improving the quality of higher education, which has been pointed out earlier. Hence, private agencies have a definitive role to play in this regard provided their support systems are harnessed suitably.

Now, several well-established educational agencies in Kerala have the required strength, capacity and capability like experienced management, involvement of committed professionals, long-standing experience in imparting technical and professional education, strong international brand names, and teams of qualified and dedicated staff who are willing to support them. Hence, they may be encouraged to develop International Higher Academic Zones/ Academic City in the State. Such institutions should be earmarked and suitably induced to evolve into landmark institutions in the country, competing and ranking with the best in the world.

Of course, the establishment of IHAZs/Academic City will not be an excuse for the State to withdraw from the field of higher education altogether. On the other hand, the State Government actually needs to step up its investment in its universities and other higher academic institutions, so as to ensure that it continues to attract the best teachers and students.

At this juncture, it is worth underscoring the fact that when importance is given to fields of higher education like engineering and technology, medical sciences, nano sciences and the like, equal significance needs to be imparted to furthering studies in fundamental sciences alongside humanizing fields of social sciences and the humanities. The pursuit of arts and culture studies should find a significant space in the curricula. Communication skills, alongside other such augmenting life-skills, should be extended a central space in the curriculum. Continued involvement of the State would ensure equilibrium and excellence in all such areas and measures.

There is some rising concern that private investments in the field of higher education would mean just two things—a dilution of human values in education and the rise of inordinate profit-based activities and involvements. Education, it needs to be noted, can certainly be seen as an investment— an investment of a different order, in terms of values for the future of humanity, but when it is merely commoditized and marketed it tends to lose its very essence. Commodity is of course something to be consumed as such and it does not allow for dialogue or discourse. It could happen that the major justification for education—knowledge generated through interaction of teacher and student in a given system—might be completely laid aside in view of the capital invested and profit generated. The academic body envisaged as providing directions to these innovations would ensure that such lapses do not occur.

On a similar note, the very concepts of IHAZs/Academic City as they are now visualized are self-supportive and income-generating. This might imply large levy of fees from the students to meet operational and functional costs. Having thus far been used to a subsidized fee structure in governmental and aided institutions, many students may not prefer to do courses in the IHAZ/ Academic City on account of their relatively higher fee. However, a sustainable revenue model needs to be developed, based on consultations with all those involved in the process, including the higher-education scholarship funds to be generated from the student fee as mentioned earlier which could ensure a more inclusive and student-friendly approach.

Many critics of privatization of education in India have pointed out that commoditization of education may lead to excessive emphasis on mere skill, a vocational and corporate-oriented education, at the severe cost of neglecting the basic sciences, humanities and the vast pool of traditional knowledge, thereby creating an imbalance among various streams of learning. This is certainly a very important point—primarily because when we rally for private enterprise in education in the lines of Dubai Academic City or such similar structures, we might stand to lose sight of the long history of education and its systems in our part of the world. Therefore, any effort to modify our higher education through the combined efforts of any outside agency needs necessarily to take an integrated approach—linking the past, present and future systems of education, self-reflexively recognizing its mode and methodology. The Government of Kerala is quite aware of this issue and due attention would be extended to this.

Yet another concern would be for providing access to the marginalized sections. An inclusive policy will be adopted so as to mete out the benefits to economically deprived segments, women, transgenders and other vulnerable sections of society.

In the end, when it comes to educational innovations, it is important to distinguish between those who seek to establish a fine balance between quality and profitability, in terms of a philanthropic measure and those that are there just for the finances involved. Here, as elsewhere, the statutory bodies through the ACA will ensure quality and accountability through periodical monitoring of the institutions. After all, education is an investment for the future—a great investment ensuring societal harmony and the survival of humanity.

BIBLIOGRAPHY

British Council. *Postgraduate student mobility trends to 2024*. https://www.britishcouncil.org/sites/default/files/postgraduate mobility trends 2024-october-14.pdf

British Council. *The Indian States Opportunities for International Higher Education Collaboration* www.britishcouncil.org/education/ihe January 2015

British Council. *Understanding India: The Future of Higher Education and Opportunities for International Cooperation.* February 2014.

CII. *Taking Stock: A sector-wide scan of Higher Education in India.* Confederation of Indian Industry and Education Sector Practice.https://www.pwc.in/assets/pdfs/industries/education/publication/higher-education-report-nov-2012.pdf

Emerging Opportunities for Private and Foreign Participation in Higher Education. file:///C:/Users/asus/Downloads/Primer 30 March Final.pdf

FICCI. *Higher Education in India: Moving towards Global Relevance and Competitiveness.* FICCI Higher Education Summit. 2014. http://www.ficci.com/spdocument/20513/FICCI-EYReport2014.pdf

FICCI. *Higher Education in India: Vision 2030.* FICCI Higher Education Summit 2013.http://www.ev.com/Publication/vwLUAssets/Higher-education-in-India-Vision-2030/$FILE/EY-Higher-education-in-India-Vision-2030.pdf

Kerala State Planning Board. *Economic Review Report 2013-14.* http://planningcommission.nic.in/plans/stateplan/Presentations13 14 /Kerala2013 14.pdf

Report of the Committee on Autonomy of Colleges in Kerala: KSHEC: 2013

Report of the Committee on Autonomy of Higher Education Institutions, constituted by the Central Advisory Board of Education (CABE) under Ministry of HRD Govt. of India.

Report of the Committee to Study the Feasibility of Establishing Private Universities in Kerala. KSHEC 2015.

Sharma, Brahm. 'India: A Lucrative Destination for FDI in Higher Education'. *International Journal of Marketing, Financial Services & Management Research.* Vol. 1 Issue 8, August 2012. http://indianresearchiournals.com/pdf/IJMFSMR/2012/August/4.pdf

TP Sreenivasan. *Higher Education in Kerala: A Way Forward.* KSHEC 2012.

UGC. *Higher Education in India at a Glance*. February 2012.

http://mhrd.gov.in/sites/upload files/mhrd/files/statistics/FSI2014 0.pdf

http://www.kshec.kerala.gov.in/images/documents/pvt%2 0utv%20final.pdf

https://www.britishcouncil.org/sites/default/files/the indian_states_oppurtunities _for _international_higher_education_col_.pdf https://www.pwc.in/assets/pdfs/publications-2010/report with ias logo.pdf India: Higher Education sector Opportunities for Foreign Universities.

https://www.pwc.in/assets/pdfs/industries/education/publication/indi a-higher-edu-sector-(251012).pdf

https://www.britishcouncil.in/sites/default/files/understanding india.pdf

www.britishcouncil.org/education/iheJanuary 2015.

ANNEX 20

Global Education Meet, Kerala 2016

[Kovalam Declaration on Making Kerala a Hub of International Education]

The Government of Kerala and the Kerala State Higher Education Council (KSHEC) organized, with the support of the Federation of Indian Chambers of Commerce and Industry (FICCI), a Global Education Meet (GEM) at Kovalam, Kerala, on 29 and 30 January 2016, which brought together over a hundred academicians, academic administrators and education providers from around the world.

The Meet, having debated various aspects relating to enhancing the international collaboration of higher education institutions (HEIs) in Kerala, for establishing an Academic City and International Higher Academic Zones, in five sessions over two days, has agreed to issue the following Declaration as the consolidated outcome of the Global Education Meet, 2016.

The Global Education Meet, 2016

Noting that there is a considerable increase in the number of students going abroad from India and other developing countries to developed countries in pursuit of higher education.

Acknowledging that international education has immense potential to enhance employability of students, improve their economic situation and help them to become world-class entrepreneurs.

Taking into consideration the high cost of international education, which allows only stakeholders from affluent families to afford the same.

Considering that a large proportion of the students who go abroad do not return to India and are thus unable to contribute to our growing economy with their skills.

Understanding that the Make in India, Digital India and other campaigns of the Government of India will benefit from an internationally trained workforce, which is able to establish and work in state-of-the-art facilities.

Expressing concern that there is no support system for economically and socially backward students to benefit from the opportunities for international education.

Acknowledging that India itself could be an attractive destination for higher education for students from many developing countries, particularly in Asia and Africa.

Taking into account the fact that the private sector has played a big role in expanding educational facilities in Kerala within the existing policy framework.

Noting that the Government of India is reported to have proposed to establish ten private universities with substantial institutional freedom to design curriculum and implement academic innovations.

Addressing the need to strengthen interdisciplinary learning and research skills into the curriculum.

Considering that universities and educational institutions in Kerala have already established a number of international collaboration programmes for student exchange, faculty exchange and research with universities abroad.

Noting that the Government of Kerala, in its budget for the year 2015-16, announced its intention to establish an Academic City and International Higher Academic Zones in Kerala.

Taking note of the success made by Academic Cities in the Middle East and Southeast Asia to attract international universities to establish their campuses in those countries.

Appreciating that a number of individuals and institutions from Kerala have expressed interest in investing in International Higher Academic Zones.

Recalling that the UN Sustainable Development Goals calls for greater efforts for international co-operation on education.

Taking into account that KSHEC has identified infrastructure, use of technology, teachers' training, research, autonomy and internationalization as areas for immediate attention in shaping a 'Higher Education 2.0' for the 21st century and has submitted 17 reports to the Government with appropriate recommendations.

Noting that the Government of Kerala has constituted an International Relations Group (IRG) to promote cooperation between the universities in Kerala and foreign universities.

Acknowledging that KSHEC has framed an IT@Colleges Programme to improve connectivity in colleges.

Noting that the KSHEC has submitted a Report, recommending that private universities should be established.

Taking note of the Thiruvananthapuram Declaration (www.kshec.gov.in) of the Meet on Transnational Education 2014, which contains valuable recommendations for promoting internationalization of higher education.

Noting with appreciation the initiative taken by the Government of Kerala to continue with its effort to promote internationalization of education by calling a GEM, which provided a platform for all participants to understand and deliberate on the opportunities and challenges posed by technology-enabled transnational education.

Noting that the present procedure for academic travel is cumbersome and not conducive to faculty and student exchanges.

Taking note of the fact that China has the third largest foreign student population in the world and it is the country that sends out the largest number students abroad.

Requests

1. The Government of India to finalize the Higher Education Bill so that a long-term legislative framework for international cooperation on education is available for educational providers to make long-term financial commitments needed for international academic cooperation.
2. The Government of India to facilitate international student exchanges by increasing the number of fellowships available for cultural exchange programmes as well as rationalizing legislation to make students entry procedures easier.

3. The Government of India to relax legislation regarding short-term employment of faculty and researchers from other countries in India which is urgently needed for the smooth functioning of the International Higher Academic Zones and other academic collaboration.
4. The Government of India to ensure massification of education with equity.
5. The Government of India to liberalize its visa regime to facilitate academic mobility.
6. The Government of India to liberalize academic travel and to eliminate redtapism in dealing with request for travel.
7. Acknowledges the pioneer efforts of International Institute for Scientific and Academic Collaboration to facilitate two batches of American students for a semester each in the university of Kerala and encourages the institute and the university of Kerala to expand and strengthen the programme.
8. The Government of Kerala to set up an Academic City Authority as a facilitator-cum-regulator for the bodies proposed to be established to promote internationalization of higher education in Kerala.
9. To transform the research landscape in the State, including through partnerships with industries and maximize the benefits of research by advancing fundamental knowledge to contribute much to the society at large.
10. To harness and align different knowledge domains and thus create Centres of Excellence which will combine inquiry and investigation.
11. The University Grants Commission to urgently streamline procedures and extend support for facilitating international

collaboration so that all institutions desirous of establishing such cooperation can do that within the shortest possible time.

12. The All India Council for Technical Education (AICTE) and other apex bodies on higher education in India to establish procedures for international recognition of Indian degrees and vice versa so as to promote internationalization of higher education in India.
13. To create an environment for blended learning which will integrate online materials, traditional classroom teaching and online virtual classrooms.
14. The Government of Kerala to finalize legislation on the establishment of an Academic City and International Higher Academic Zones so as to give a boost to internationalization of education in the State.
15. The Government of Kerala to initiate work to identify locations for an Academic City and to approve the locations for International Higher Academic Zones as identified by academic providers so that individuals and institutions desirous of partnering can start to prepare their plans.
16. The Government of Kerala to make available procedures and incentives for faculty and students in the Academic City and International Higher Academic Zones.
17. The Government of Kerala to implement the report of the KSHEC on establishing private universities in Kerala at the earliest.
18. The Government of Kerala to ensure that economically and socially weaker sections of the society have access to the new institutions, courses and opportunities created in the Academic City and International Higher Academic Zones.

19. The Government of Kerala to establish procedures which will ensure gender equality in access to the new institutions, courses and opportunities created in the Academic City and International Higher Academic Zones.
20. The Kerala State Higher Education Council to arrange training programmes for managers of higher educational institutions in Kerala on legal and practical aspects of establishing international collaboration, including student and faculty exchange.
21. The Department of Higher Education, Government of Kerala, to support educational institutions in the State to establish 100% high speed connectivity with data network in every academic institution so that students can benefit from technologically enhanced learning on the basis of the Report on IT@Colleges.
22. The universities in the State to revise their rules and regulations to facilitate exchange of faculty, student and researchers locally, nationally and internationally in a seamless manner.
23. The universities in the State to urgently establish easy and transparent procedures for international academic credit recognition to support student exchange programmes.
24. The universities in the State to take full advantage of technologically enhanced learning by promoting Massive Open Online Courses (MOOCs), flipped classrooms and blended learning in their universities.
25. The Academic institutions in the State, both in public sector and private sector, to start to work on international collaborations for teaching, research, student and faculty exchange so as to get familiarized with international cooperation which will be greatly expanded in the coming years.

26. The Public and Private Sector Companies in Kerala to consider contributing in higher education including research as part of their corporate social responsibility to contribute to a sustainable State.
27. The Individuals and companies owned and promoted by Indians abroad to invest in the Academic City and International Higher Academic Zones in Kerala.
28. The faculty members in academic institutions in the State to proactively engage international academic community for collaborative research, teaching and student exchange to maximize internationalization of curriculum and educational experience.
29. The student community in the State to see the internationalization of higher education as a huge opportunity to be exposed to higher education of global standards, which will improve their ability to pursue higher education and research.
30. The student community to take advantage of internationalization of education as a way to maximize their employability locally and globally.
31. The educational providers in Kerala to leverage Kerala's reputation as a family-friendly and economical global tourist destination to market their capacity to deliver quality higher education at affordable costs across the developing world in order to attract more international students to come to Kerala and increase diversity in classrooms.
32. Considers that good governance of educational institutions is required to ensure quality, efficiency and transparency.

The Participants of the GEM Further Resolve:

To continue the discussions individually in coming days in their respective countries, academic forums and educational institutions they represent, to harness the potential of internationalization of education

and

To promote, in their respective countries and spheres of influence, the relevant conclusions from the Thiruvananthapuram Declaration (www.kshec.kerala.gov.in) on Transnational Education 2014 and the Kovalam Declaration of the Global Education Meet 2016.

The Participants of the GEM Further Request:

The KSHEC to widely publicize the Kovalam Declaration on International Education so that students, teachers, academic policymakers, education providers and other stakeholders of higher education can use it as a basic document to advocate and promote transnational education.

The participants noted with concern the undue anxieties in certain sections about internationalization of higher education because of a lack of understanding of the concept and expressed the hope that dissent will not degenerate in to violence.

The participants of the GEM express appreciation for the Government of Kerala for the excellent arrangements for the Meet and for its generous hospitality.

[Issued in Kovalam, on 30 January 2016]

INDEX

Academia 13, 26, 49, 68, 114
Academia-Industry linkages 50
Academic calendar 33, 80, 83, 164
Academic City 8–10, 52, 182, 209, 219–28, 231, 233, 235–8
Academic City Authority (ACA) 225, 228, 235
Academic excellence 12–4, 31, 34, 44, 90, 161
Accountability 12, 38, 69, 120–21, 131, 149, 213, 228
Accreditation xvi, 27, 37–8, 40–41, 65, 79, 120, 130, 135, 145, 150, 163, 168, 170, 177, 186–7, 196, 212
Advisory Council 18, 61
Afghanistan 200
All India Council for Technical Education (AICTE) 15, 32, 204, 236
Arabic University 58, 71, 73–4
Assessment and Accreditation 37–8, 40, 120, 130, 135, 163, 168, 170
Assessment Council xvi, 150, 163, 175
Association of Indian Universities (AIU) 118
Athabasca University (Canada) 183
Australia 56, 181–2, 185, 212–3
Autonomous Colleges Scheme 35
Autonomy
    grants 34
    implementation of 35–6
Autonomy Committee 36
Awareness xvi, 13, 45, 150, 172, 198, 205, 215, 221

Backward classes 14
Bar Council of India 16
Bar Council of Kerala xviii
Bhagawati, Jagdish 138
Bill of Rights for Women 68
BJP 6–7, 156
Board of Studies 27–9, 34
Bureaucracy xv, xvii, 22, 46, 62, 66–7, 165

Caledonian University, UK 181
Calicut 93, 102, 163
Calicut University 93, 102
Canada 56, 182–3, 213
CCNA 180
Centrally Sponsored Scheme (CSS) 63
Centre for Capacity Building 15
Centre for Policy and Developmental Studies and Statistical Analysis 81
Centre for Research on Policies in Higher Education 15
Certification Programmes 177, 180
Chandy, Oommen, Chief Minister of Kerela xviii, 1, 5, 20, 46
Chennai 31, 149, 153
Chennithala, Ramesh, Home Minister 20, 59
China 116, 182, 185, 212, 234
Choice-Based Credit and Semester System (CBCSS) 25, 27–8, 170–71
Choice-Based Credit System (CBCS) 25, 162, 167
CII Conference on Innovation in Higher Education 128
Civic organisations 7
Civil disobedience 60
Clinton, Hillary 119
Cochin College 98
Cochin University of Science and Technology (CUSAT) 44, 102, 118, 156

Codes of ethics 4
College Academic Council 34
College Clustering 163
College Cluster Multiple Campus Universities (CCMCU) 79, 163
Colleges
  aided 35, 86, 97, 149, 153, 169
  Arabic 71
  autonomous xvi, 31–4, 36, 64, 150, 154, 160–61, 163, 172, 174
  demand for access and expansion of 32
  formation of clusters of 97
  government 35, 97, 211
  professional 64, 78
  setting up of cluster of 99
  sports and cultural activities in 16
Columbia University 138
Competitiveness 45, 133, 140, 186
Computer labs 87
Conference in Education 147
Conference of Vice-Chancellors, Kochi 118
Congress Party 6, 21
Connectivism and Connective Knowledge (CCK08) 183
Continuous Quality Improvement Plan (CQIP) 40
Corporate or institutional social responsibility (CSR) 223
Corruption 90, 98, 152
Council Secretariat 22
CSIR 221
Culture xv, 69, 78, 109, 115, 119, 142, 159, 218, 227
  ethics and xv
Curriculum Development Centre 15
Curtin University 181

DBT 221
Decoupling 177, 187
Democracy 3, 5, 121
  militant 3, 5
  threat to 3
Department of Higher Education xvii, 8–9, 21, 46, 59, 64, 66–7, 91–2, 101–2, 169, 171, 225, 237
  International Relations Group 91
Digitization 223
Diplomacy xv, 107, 113, 123, 173
Distance Education Council, Delhi 77
Distance Learning Programmes 177, 180
DIT 221
DST 221
Dubai Academic City 52, 182, 228

East Africa 54, 224
Economy 53, 73, 116, 157, 196, 211–2, 224, 232
Education
  autonomy and accountability 12, 120
  changes in xvi, 172, 175
  commercialisation of 4–6, 35, 76
  commoditizing of 142
  impact of globalization on 140–41
  infrastructure xv, 5, 23, 48, 64–5, 78, 80, 86, 111, 129, 132–3, 142, 145, 149, 152, 159, 167, 169–70, 174, 192, 194–5, 197, 201–2, 233
  internationalization of 138–9, 144, 178, 234, 236, 238–9
  liberalization and deregulation of 142
  massification, internationalization and marketization of 120
  methods of 124
  new policy for 223
  planning or funding 48
  policy formulation and perspective planning 12
  privatisation of 35
  privatization of 140, 228
  quality of 14, 41–2, 58, 77, 132, 140–41, 162, 201, 219, 221
  reform of 24
  research and internationalisation xvi, 5, 23
  revolution 5, 161, 173, 190, 201
  standards of 32
  technical and professional 56, 226
  technology-based xvi
  training of teachers and administrative staff xv–vi, 5, 149, 151, 202, 233
  transnational 150, 178–80, 182, 200–205, 207–8, 218, 234, 239
  Western 120–21
  World-class 118
Educational software 14
Education Conference, IIT Delhi 138
Education for the Future 95, 150, 206
Efficiency 31, 87, 152, 238

e-learning 14, 78, 86
Employment and Global Skills Development Cell 15
Enrollments 55
Entry examination equivalency 101
Ernakulam 97, 98
Erudite Programme 100–101
Ethics xv, 4, 78, 162, 193
Europe 56, 120, 179
European Credit Transfer System 205
Examination calendar 83
Examination Reforms Cell 15
Executive Council xvii, xviii, 18, 22, 41, 84–5, 94, 107, 112, 115
  Inaugural Address at the First Session of the 107
Exploitation 69, 128

Faculty Academy xvi, 162, 167, 175
  establishment of 162
Faculty Exchange/Visiting Scholars/Sabbatical Professorships 217
Federation of Indian Chambers of Commerce and Industry (FICCI) 9, 231
Fee sharing 101
Financial assistance 14, 102
Foreign universities xvii, 8–10, 24, 29, 51–2, 119, 135, 141, 202, 218
France 182, 200
Freeships 14

Gender 16, 45, 68–70, 121, 237
  discrimination 69
  equality 68, 237
  issues 16, 69
  justice 68
  sensitisation 45, 69–70
General Agreement on Trade in Services (GATS) 212
Germany 185, 199–200
Global Education Meet (GEM), 2016 1, 4–5, 9–11, 209–10, 219, 231, 234, 239
  agenda of 9, 219
  Inaugural Session of 4
  inauguration session of 4
  recommendations 5
  reform proposals 8
  success of 10
Globalization 5, 9, 137–42, 161, 173, 215
Global Meet 8
Global Universities Partnership on Environment and Sustainability (GUPES) 202, 207
Gopakumar, G xviii
Gopinath, Meenakshi xviii, 31, 68, 147

Harassment 69–70
Higher education
  access and equity in 32
  aspects of xvii, 17
  autonomy and innovations in 38
  challenges in 132, 138
  commercialisation of 4
  concepts and programmes in 12, 85
  curriculum and syllabi 14
  decision-making process in 19
  development of 13, 148
  equity in 77, 79
  facilities in 13
  financial sustainability of 54
  funding agencies 14, 217
  generation and utilisation of funds 14
  grading/mark system 27
  growth of 12–3
  ills of 43
  impact on 23
  importance in 16
  inclusion and excellence in 56
  innovative courses and research projects 54
  institutions 13–4, 17, 37–8, 48, 63, 69, 128, 130, 213, 231
    functioning of 38
  institutions of 12–6, 39, 69
  language of 29
  needs of xvii, 23
  opportunities for 14
  policy for 13, 15, 75
  politicisation of 23
  private investment in 8, 53, 224
  problems of 43, 103
  quality of 8, 35, 37, 42, 56, 78, 80, 82, 118, 122, 133, 163, 204, 223, 226
    Assurance Framework for 38
    evaluation and assessment 120
    growth of 82
    improvement in 44
  reform in xvii, 8, 11, 85, 152

requirement for 85
recommendations for 75
implementation of 21, 135
regulatory agencies 12, 17
role of the private sector and foreign universities 24
Semester System xvi, 25–8, 30, 136, 145, 164, 167, 172, 174, 216, 213, 235
transnational 212
trends in 43, 96, 164
Higher Education 2.0 xvi, 5, 8, 23, 145–6, 149, 156, 161, 172, 174, 202, 233
Higher Education 3.0 174
Higher Education Council (HEC) xv, 4–5, 9, 11–2, 107, 118, 120, 124, 130, 143, 149, 151–2, 155, 169–71, 200, 205–8, 210, 231, 237
Higher Education Department 17, 22, 151
Higher Education Institution (HEI) 38–9, 68–70, 231
Open Forum of Stakeholders in 69
Hoarding 6
Home Affairs and External Affairs 92
Hridayakumari 25, 27
Hridayakumari Report 27
Human depravity 8
Human Resource Development (HRD) 13, 17, 46, 50, 92, 119, 159, 169, 210
planning 13
Human resources 13, 56
qualified and dedicated 56
Human Resources Development 15
Human rights 45, 78

ICAR 221
ICT 45, 162, 174, 217
ICT-Enabled Joint Teaching 217
IIMs 61, 154, 197
IKKM 147
India IT Summit, Thiruvananthapuram 123
Indian Council for Cultural Relations (ICCR) 218
Indian Education Congress 2015, New Delhi, on 'Graduates of the 21st Century' 173
Indian Education Service 88
Indian Express 159
Article on Education 159
Indian Institutes of Technology (IIT) 61, 110, 114, 119, 138, 145–6, 154, 197, 199
India semester programme for foreign students xvi
Industrial revolution 5
Industry 48–9, 54, 79, 114, 116, 123–6, 128, 130, 133, 135, 145, 199, 214
Infrastructure
academic 48
lack of 70
Innovativeness 27
Institution-Industry Interface 114
Institutions
academic 48, 181–2, 186–7, 195, 203–4, 226, 238
commercial 141
educational 56–7, 63, 70, 114, 124, 131, 133, 138, 148–9, 197, 201, 207, 213, 220, 223, 226, 233, 237–9
governance of 238
state-run 56, 226
higher education 13–4, 17, 37–8, 48, 63, 69, 128, 130, 213, 231
quality of 39
research 13, 16, 79, 160, 221
State-level 16
International Branch Campus (IBCs) 177, 181–3, 201, 205
International Conference on Transnational Education 9, 57
International Dual-Degree Programme 215
International Higher Academic Zones (IHAZs) 209, 219–27, 231, 233, 235–8
International Higher Education Zones 9–10, 57
International Integrated Dual-Degree Programme 216
International Meet on Transnational Education 51, 95, 155, 176, 200, 202, 206–8
International Relations Group (IRG) 101, 202, 233
International Student Exchange Programme 216
International Twining Programme 216
Internet 124, 126, 133–4, 139–40, 177, 182, 190, 195

Islam 72, 73
IT
  equipment 85, 87
  facilities 86
  industry 49, 123–6, 133
  professionals 123–4, 126
  revolution 123, 125, 127, 173
IT@Colleges Committee 86
IT@Colleges Programme 202, 233
Iyer, Pico 125, 127

James, Jancy xviii
Jasintha Quadras 31
Jayaprakash, R 37, 91
Job-seekers 49
Jobs, Steve 116
Joint Conferences/Seminars/Workshops/Training Programmes 217
Joint Research Collaboration 217
Joseph, Babu 44
Justice Verma Committee Report 68

Kakkanadan 147
Kalpatha 2011 113
Kannur University 102, 119
Keltron 98
Kenya 200
Kerala
  colleges in 31, 33, 86, 151, 211
  development 13
  economy of 73, 196
  educational agencies in 56, 226
  higher education in xv, 5, 20, 36, 38, 42–3, 48, 86, 103, 107–8, 110, 112, 123, 129, 144, 147, 152, 162, 201, 211, 235
  IT initiatives in 86
  LDF Government 36, 62, 170
  operation of private universities in xvi
  social development 13
  socio-economic requirements of 12
  strengths and weaknesses of xv
  UDF Government 8, 20, 62
  universities in xvi, 10, 22, 51–3, 55, 57, 80, 82–3, 102, 147, 151, 202, 206, 233, 236
Kerala Club 147
Kerala High Court 1, 6
Kerala Higher Education Council 4
Kerala Legislative Assembly 12, 132
Kerala State Assessment and Accreditation Council (KSAAC) xvi, 37–42, 79, 150, 170–72
  activities of 38
  assessment procedures of 39, 41
  Executive Committee of 39
  vision and mission of 38
Kerala State Higher Education Council (KSHEC)
  achievement of xvi, 171
  administrative control of 46
  functions and responsibilities of the 85
  objective of 167
  provisions of 38
  recommendations 45
  responsibilities of 12
  supervision of 45
Kerala State Higher Education Council (KSHEC) Act, 2007 80
Kerala State Library Network (KSLNET) 78
Kerala Travels 6
Kerala University 20, 102, 133, 199
Knowledge Commission Report 37, 75
Kochi xviii, 118, 128, 156, 163
Kovalam 2–3, 9–11, 210, 231, 239
Kovalam Declaration 3, 11, 210, 231, 239
Kovalam incident 9
Kozhikode 97
KPCC 20

Languages xv, 8, 28–9, 71, 73–4, 107, 109, 126, 135, 157, 180, 195, 202–3
  Arabic 58, 71–4, 150
  English 109, 135, 180, 195
  Malayalam 72–3, 110, 147, 150, 199, 205
  Tamil 72
Law 61, 68, 191, 193
Learning
  experiential and service 54
  personalisation of 54
  personalised 54
  student-centric 32
  technology-based 23
Leela Hotel, Kovalam 2
Left Democratic Front (LDF) 25, 36, 62, 170
Leftists 3, 4, 6

Leonardo da Vinci 117
Lethargy xvi, xvii, 89, 152, 161
Liberalisation 90, 92
Library 78, 85, 111, 197, 221
Linkages 10, 13, 16, 48, 50, 52, 57, 114, 145, 152, 159, 161
  international 57, 152, 159
Literacy rates 69
Lokayukta of Kerala 7

Macaulay 124
Madhava Menon, NR xviii, 31, 59, 147
Malayala Manorama 3
Malaysia 56, 181–2, 198
Manipulation 11, 22
Maoist/Naxalite movement 60
Mappilas 72
Martyrs' Memorial 7
Massive Open Online Courses (MOOCs) 86, 150, 156–7, 159–60, 166, 174, 177–8, 183–90, 192–3, 197, 201, 203, 205–6, 237
  acceptance of 186, 193
Mathai, Samuel 20
Mathew 2, 153–4
Mathrubhumi 5
Media 3, 26, 68, 213
Medical Council of India 16
Mediocrity 152, 161
Meet on Transnational Education 2014 234
Menon, KPS 108
Microsoft 124
Middle East 71–2, 198–9, 233
Migration 49, 140, 212
Ministry of External Affairs 22
Ministry of Human Resource Development (MHRD) 17, 50, 63–5, 69, 148, 169, 171, 210, 225
Minorities 79
Misogyny 70
Mistrust 99
MK Nambyar Academy for Continuing Legal Education, Kochi xviii
Mohandas, K 91
Multinational corporations (MNCs) 205
Muslim League 57

Narayana Guru 136
Narayana Murthy Committee 141, 146
Narayanan, Shri KR 108
Narayana Pillai, MP 147
National Accreditation Council 27
National Assessment and Accreditation Council (NAAC) 37–8, 41–2, 120, 163, 168
National Council for Teacher Education 16
National Examination Board on Occupational Safety and Health (NEBOSH) 181
National Institute for Technology (Canada) in Liberal Education 183
National Judicial Academy 82
National Research Council (Canada) 183
National Seminar in 2012 23, 31
National University for Police Sciences and Security Studies (NUPSAS) 60–61
National University of Educational Planning and Administration, New Delhi xviii
NCC 28
Nepal 200
Netherlands 200
New Caledonian College in Oman 181
New York Times 125
NGOs 68
Non-Resident Keralites 73
NSS 28

OBC 79
Online Courses 86, 156, 159, 177, 182–3, 185–6, 189–90, 201, 205, 237
Open Educational Resources (OER) 183
Organised crime 60

Panikkar, Dr KN 108
Panikkar, Sardar KM 108
Parthasarathy, Anand 86
Parthasarathy, Shri G. 108
Patil, Jagannath 37
Pillai, Chandrasekharan 82
Planning Commission 141
Plato's Academy 131
Police Science University 65
Police Studies and Forensic Sciences 150
Police University 59, 61, 170–71
Political
  expediency 23
  interferences 82
  leaders 11
  will 76

Pondicherry University 111, 209
Prathap, Gangan 93
Pravasi Bharatiya Divas 128
Primary education 44, 214
Private Sector Organisations 204
Private universities xvi, 8–10, 51–8, 151, 206, 211, 232, 234, 236
 advantages of 53
Privatisation 3, 35
Professionalism 44, 110
Professor UR Ananthmurthy Committee 75
Professor Yash Pal Committee Report on Higher Education 75
Programmes for Gender Sensitisation on Campuses 68
Public-private partnership (PPP) 77, 141, 219
Punnoose, Jacob, former DGP 59

Rabb, Abdu, Education Minister of Kerela xviii
Rashtriya Uchchatar Shiksha Abhiyan (RUSA) 22, 63–7, 148–9, 151, 153, 159, 163, 165, 169–71, 175
 administration of 171
Rediff.com 4
Regional separatism movements 60
Regulatory bodies 12, 15, 32, 204
Report on Autonomous Colleges in Kerala 167
Report on Kerala State Assessment and Accreditation Council 168
Report on Kerala State Faculty Academy 167
Research and development (R&D) 32, 114–5, 139, 221–2
Research and Innovation University 65

SAKSHAM Report on 'Measures for Ensuring the Safety of Women 68–9
Samaagati Report 68, 70
Scheduled Castes (SC) 14, 79
Scheduled Tribes (ST) 14, 79
Scholarship 14, 100, 108, 148, 171, 217, 228
Secondary education 44, 214
Sectarianism 152
Self-evaluation 38
Self-financing institutions 10, 80
Self-seeking manoeuvre 22
Self-study report 39, 40
Seminar on Autonomy Sacred Heart College 153
Sen, Amartya 174
Sheikh Zainuddin Makhdoom 72
Singapore 56, 143, 198
Skills
 analytical 45
 communication 45, 145, 162
 computer networking 180
 development 151, 174
 diplomatic 21
 entrepreneurial 45
 graduate employability 41
 pedagogic 162
 teaching 44
Smart Classrooms 86
Social inequality 141
Social justice 12–4, 16, 45
 commitment to 45
 objectives of 14, 16
 promotion of 13
Solar Commission 1
South Asia 54, 198, 224
South-South collaboration 202, 207
Sports and arts 28
Sports Development Academy 78
Sreenivasan, TP
 16 Reports submitted to the Government 23
 Address to the Conference of Vice-Chancellors, Kochi 118
 as Ambassador 5, 6, 8
 as Vice Chairman of the Kerala State Higher Education Council (KSHEC) xv, 20
 as Vice Chairman of the Organising Committee 10
 attack by SFI 3–5, 7
  condemnation of 3, 7
 insult and violence 3
Srinivasan, Rajeev 4, 49
State Accreditation Council 168
State Council for Assessment of Higher Education Institutions 15, 17
State Higher Educational Tribunal 79
State Higher Education Council xv, 5, 11–2, 107, 118, 120, 143, 149, 155, 169, 200, 205–8, 210, 231, 237

State Higher Education Policy 75
State Sports Training Centre 78
State University for Distance Education (Open University) 77, 110, 194
Student Federation of India (SFI) 3–6
Student visa 101
Study Abroad Programme 216
Summer/Winter Schools 216
Sustainable Development decade 204
Sustainable Development Goals 201, 204, 233
Swami Vivekananda 6, 109, 136
Sweden 200
Switzerland 182, 200
Syllabi and textbooks 14, 26, 28–9, 34, 134

Tareen, JAK xviii, 75, 111
Teachers
- assessment of 88
- incentives for 88
- training xv–vi, 5, 17, 23, 149, 151, 202, 233

Teaching
- aids 44, 45
- material 14, 191
- methods of 44, 53, 129, 133, 164, 210
- personnel 14, 26, 43, 83
  - short-term courses to train and update 14
- standards for 44
- technology-based 23

Technocapitalism 125
Technoculture 125
Technology xvi, 5, 23, 33, 49, 54, 85–6, 90, 98, 115, 124, 130–31, 133, 140, 149–50, 152, 154, 159–60, 164, 166–7, 170, 174–6, 190, 201–4, 212, 219, 221, 226, 233–4
- use of 85–6, 98, 131, 133, 149, 152, 166–7, 170, 174–5, 202, 233

Technology Enhanced Learning and Teaching (TELT) 86
Technopark 113
TED 150, 160, 166
Thiruvananthapuram 4, 7, 9, 45, 51, 57, 97, 99, 123, 155, 176, 200, 206–8, 234, 239
Thiruvananthapuram Declaration 9, 51, 57, 200, 207, 234, 239
Thiruvananthapuram International Meet on Transnational Education 200
Thomas, Cyriac 52
Thomas, Justice Sunil 6
Thoreau, Henry David 127
Thrissur 1, 52
Thummarukudy, Muralee 176, 199
Tierney, Prof. William 5
Times of India, The 5
TOEFL 180
Training
- induction 45
- in-service 43–4
- professional 44, 48, 54, 162, 224
- programmes 54, 134, 150, 166, 171–2, 217, 237
- staff 78
- teachers xv, 5, 149, 151, 202, 233

Transfer of credit 101
Transgenders 228
Transnational Education (TNE) 51, 176–83, 185, 193–8, 206
- definitions of 179
- models 183
- types of 180

Trivandrum 163
Twinning 177, 181, 183, 219

UDACITY 184–5, 188–9
UNC-India Summit II at the University of North Carolina at Chapel Hill 155
UN Decade of Education for Sustainable Development 207
Unemployment 49
UNESCO 115, 162, 179, 201
UNESCO Policy Forum 115
United Democratic Front (UDF) 8, 20, 25, 62
United Kingdom (UK) 56, 120, 181–2, 185, 200, 212–3
United Nations 176, 199–200, 202–3, 207
United Nations Environment Programme (UNEP) 176, 199, 202, 207
United Nations University 199
United States of America (USA) 56, 119–21, 144, 157, 176, 182, 185, 200, 212–3
Universities
- academic freedom and autonomy to 82

autonomy of 16, 27, 79, 80, 120
availability of funds 76, 171
capacities of 32
demand for access and expansion of 32
funds 83, 108
governance of the 79
international 219–20, 223, 233
research and teaching standards 76
Statutes, Ordinances and Regulations of the 14
teacher-administrators in 13
unification of syllabi 26
uniform act for 82
Universities Act 80
University Appellate Tribunal 83
University Grants Commission (UGC) 12, 15, 17, 27, 32–6, 51, 68–9, 77–8, 83–4, 97, 118, 163, 203–4, 210, 225, 235
teacher-student ratio 78, 134
University Grants Commission (UGC) Guidelines 33, 35
University of Manitoba, Canada 183

Vice Chairman xv, 10, 18, 20, 102
Vice Chancellors 18, 20–22, 26–7, 70, 80, 84
qualifications of 84
Videsha Vicharam 4
Vijayan, OV 147
Violence 2–3, 6, 69–70, 239
cult of 3, 6
gender-based 69–70
politics of 3
Virtual Labs 86

West Asia 54, 224
Women 69–70, 77, 228
prejudices against 69
Women Empowerment Cells 69
Workshops and seminars 15–6, 69–70
World Economic Summit 5
World Trade Organization (WTO) 212

Zuckerberg, Mark 116